50 Southern American Recipes for Home

By: Kelly Johnson

Table of Contents

- Fried chicken
- Shrimp and grits
- Southern-style biscuits and gravy
- Jambalaya
- Chicken and waffles
- Hush puppies
- Shrimp po'boy sandwich
- Collard greens
- Gumbo
- Fried green tomatoes
- Pimento cheese
- Red beans and rice
- Buttermilk pie
- Cornbread
- Sweet tea
- Pulled pork barbecue
- Fried catfish
- Cajun shrimp boil
- Peach cobbler
- Biscuits with sausage gravy
- Crawfish étouffée
- Blackened fish
- Southern-style macaroni and cheese
- Banana pudding
- Chicken fried steak
- Shrimp and okra gumbo
- Pecan pie
- Barbecue ribs
- Chicken and dumplings
- Grits with cheese
- Cornbread dressing
- Beignets
- Bourbon-glazed ham
- Shrimp and sausage jambalaya
- Key lime pie

- Shrimp and grits casserole
- Fried okra
- Boudin sausage
- Cajun dirty rice
- Sweet potato pie
- Texas chili
- Southern-style coleslaw
- Gooey butter cake
- Cajun fried turkey
- Chicken bog
- Chocolate pecan pie
- Brunswick stew
- Fried pickles
- Cheese grits with shrimp
- BBQ pulled chicken

Fried chicken

Ingredients:

- 8 pieces of chicken (legs, thighs, breasts, or wings)
- 2 cups buttermilk
- 2 cups all-purpose flour
- 1 tablespoon salt
- 1 tablespoon black pepper
- 1 tablespoon paprika
- 1 teaspoon garlic powder
- 1 teaspoon onion powder
- Vegetable oil, for frying

Instructions:

1. Prepare the Chicken:
    - Rinse the chicken pieces under cold water and pat them dry with paper towels. Season the chicken pieces with salt and pepper.
2. Marinate the Chicken:
    - Place the chicken pieces in a large bowl and pour the buttermilk over them. Make sure the chicken is completely submerged in the buttermilk. Cover the bowl and refrigerate for at least 4 hours, or overnight for best results.
3. Prepare the Coating:
    - In a shallow dish or large bowl, mix together the flour, salt, pepper, paprika, garlic powder, and onion powder until well combined.
4. Coat the Chicken:
    - Remove the chicken from the buttermilk marinade, allowing any excess buttermilk to drip off. Dredge each chicken piece in the seasoned flour mixture, coating it evenly on all sides. Shake off any excess flour.
5. Fry the Chicken:
    - In a large, deep skillet or Dutch oven, heat about 1 inch of vegetable oil over medium-high heat until it reaches 350°F (175°C).
    - Carefully place the coated chicken pieces in the hot oil, making sure not to overcrowd the pan. Fry the chicken in batches if necessary.

- Fry the chicken for about 6-8 minutes per side, or until golden brown and cooked through. The internal temperature of the chicken should reach 165°F (75°C).
- Once cooked, remove the chicken from the oil and place it on a wire rack or paper towels to drain excess oil.

6. Serve:
    - Serve the fried chicken hot, with your favorite sides such as mashed potatoes, coleslaw, biscuits, or cornbread.
    - Enjoy your homemade crispy and flavorful fried chicken!

Feel free to adjust the seasonings and spices according to your taste preferences. You can also add other herbs and spices to the flour mixture for extra flavor.

Shrimp and grits

Ingredients:

For the grits:

- 1 cup stone-ground grits
- 4 cups water or chicken broth
- Salt and pepper to taste
- 2 tablespoons unsalted butter
- 1 cup shredded sharp cheddar cheese (optional)

For the shrimp:

- 1 pound large shrimp, peeled and deveined
- Salt and pepper to taste
- 2 tablespoons olive oil
- 4 slices bacon, chopped
- 1 small onion, diced
- 1 bell pepper, diced
- 2 cloves garlic, minced
- 1 cup cherry tomatoes, halved
- 1/2 cup chicken broth
- 2 tablespoons fresh lemon juice
- 2 tablespoons chopped fresh parsley

Instructions:

1. Prepare the Grits:
   - In a medium saucepan, bring the water or chicken broth to a boil. Gradually whisk in the grits, stirring constantly to prevent lumps from forming.
   - Reduce the heat to low and simmer, stirring occasionally, until the grits are thick and creamy, about 20-25 minutes.
   - Stir in the butter and shredded cheddar cheese (if using) until melted and well combined. Season with salt and pepper to taste. Keep warm while you prepare the shrimp.

2. Cook the Shrimp:
    - Season the shrimp with salt and pepper to taste.
    - Heat the olive oil in a large skillet over medium-high heat. Add the chopped bacon and cook until crispy. Remove the bacon from the skillet and set aside.
    - In the same skillet, add the seasoned shrimp in a single layer. Cook for 2-3 minutes per side, or until pink and opaque. Remove the shrimp from the skillet and set aside.
    - In the same skillet, add the diced onion and bell pepper. Cook until softened, about 3-4 minutes. Add the minced garlic and cook for an additional 1 minute.
    - Stir in the halved cherry tomatoes, chicken broth, and fresh lemon juice. Bring the mixture to a simmer and cook for 2-3 minutes.
    - Return the cooked bacon and shrimp to the skillet. Cook for another 1-2 minutes, or until heated through.
    - Remove the skillet from the heat and stir in the chopped fresh parsley.
3. Serve:
    - Divide the creamy grits among serving bowls. Top with the shrimp and vegetable mixture.
    - Serve the shrimp and grits immediately, garnished with additional parsley if desired.
    - Enjoy your delicious and comforting shrimp and grits!

Feel free to customize this recipe by adding your favorite seasonings or vegetables. You can also adjust the consistency of the grits by adding more liquid if needed.

Southern-style biscuits and gravy

Ingredients:

For the biscuits:

- 2 cups all-purpose flour
- 1 tablespoon baking powder
- 1/2 teaspoon salt
- 1/2 cup unsalted butter, cold and cubed
- 3/4 cup buttermilk

For the sausage gravy:

- 1 pound ground breakfast sausage (pork or turkey)
- 1/4 cup all-purpose flour
- 3 cups whole milk
- Salt and pepper to taste

Instructions:

1. Make the Biscuits:
    - Preheat your oven to 425°F (220°C). Line a baking sheet with parchment paper.
    - In a large mixing bowl, whisk together the flour, baking powder, and salt.
    - Add the cold, cubed butter to the flour mixture. Use a pastry cutter or your fingertips to work the butter into the flour until it resembles coarse crumbs.
    - Make a well in the center of the mixture and pour in the buttermilk. Stir until just combined and a soft dough forms.
    - Turn the dough out onto a lightly floured surface. Pat it into a rectangle about 1/2-inch thick.
    - Use a biscuit cutter or a glass to cut out biscuits. Place the biscuits on the prepared baking sheet.
    - Gather the scraps of dough, pat them together, and cut out additional biscuits.

- Bake the biscuits in the preheated oven for 12-15 minutes, or until golden brown and cooked through.
2. Make the Sausage Gravy:
    - While the biscuits are baking, cook the ground sausage in a large skillet over medium heat, breaking it up with a spoon, until browned and cooked through.
    - Sprinkle the flour over the cooked sausage and stir to combine. Cook for 1-2 minutes, stirring constantly.
    - Gradually pour in the milk, stirring constantly to prevent lumps from forming. Continue to cook, stirring occasionally, until the gravy thickens and comes to a simmer.
    - Reduce the heat to low and simmer the gravy for 2-3 minutes, stirring occasionally, until it reaches your desired consistency. Season with salt and pepper to taste.
3. Serve:
    - Split the warm biscuits in half and place them on serving plates.
    - Ladle the hot sausage gravy over the biscuits.
    - Serve immediately and enjoy your delicious Southern-style biscuits and gravy!

Feel free to adjust the seasonings in the gravy to suit your taste preferences. You can also add a pinch of cayenne pepper for a bit of heat, or sprinkle chopped fresh parsley over the top for garnish.

Jambalaya

Ingredients:

- 1 tablespoon olive oil
- 1 pound boneless, skinless chicken thighs, cut into bite-sized pieces
- 1 pound andouille sausage, sliced
- 1 large onion, diced
- 1 bell pepper, diced
- 2 celery stalks, diced
- 3 cloves garlic, minced
- 1 can (14.5 ounces) diced tomatoes
- 1 cup long-grain white rice
- 2 cups chicken broth
- 1 teaspoon smoked paprika
- 1 teaspoon dried thyme
- 1 teaspoon dried oregano
- 1/2 teaspoon cayenne pepper (optional, for heat)
- Salt and black pepper to taste
- 1 pound medium shrimp, peeled and deveined
- 2 green onions, thinly sliced (for garnish)
- Fresh chopped parsley (for garnish)

Instructions:

1. Sauté the Meat:
    - Heat the olive oil in a large skillet or Dutch oven over medium-high heat. Add the chicken thighs and andouille sausage to the skillet. Cook, stirring occasionally, until the chicken is browned and the sausage is lightly browned, about 5-6 minutes. Remove the chicken and sausage from the skillet and set aside.
2. Sauté the Vegetables:
    - In the same skillet, add the diced onion, bell pepper, celery, and minced garlic. Cook, stirring occasionally, until the vegetables are softened, about 5 minutes.
3. Add the Rice and Spices:
    - Stir in the diced tomatoes (with their juices), long-grain white rice, chicken broth, smoked paprika, dried thyme, dried oregano, cayenne pepper (if using), salt, and black pepper. Bring the mixture to a boil.

4. Simmer:
    - Reduce the heat to low, cover the skillet, and simmer for 20-25 minutes, or until the rice is cooked and the liquid is absorbed.
5. Add the Shrimp:
    - Stir in the peeled and deveined shrimp, along with the cooked chicken and sausage. Cover and cook for an additional 5-7 minutes, or until the shrimp is pink and cooked through.
6. Serve:
    - Remove the skillet from the heat. Garnish with sliced green onions and fresh chopped parsley.
    - Serve the jambalaya hot, and enjoy!

This hearty and flavorful jambalaya is perfect for serving as a main dish for a weeknight dinner or for entertaining guests at a gathering. Adjust the seasonings and spices according to your taste preferences, and feel free to add additional vegetables or proteins if desired.

Chicken and waffles

Ingredients:

For the fried chicken:

- 4 boneless, skinless chicken breasts or thighs
- 1 cup buttermilk
- 1 cup all-purpose flour
- 1 teaspoon salt
- 1/2 teaspoon black pepper
- 1/2 teaspoon paprika
- 1/2 teaspoon garlic powder
- Vegetable oil, for frying

For the waffles:

- 2 cups all-purpose flour
- 1 tablespoon baking powder
- 1 tablespoon granulated sugar
- 1/2 teaspoon salt
- 2 large eggs
- 1 3/4 cups milk
- 1/2 cup unsalted butter, melted
- Vegetable oil or non-stick cooking spray, for waffle iron

For serving:

- Butter
- Maple syrup

Instructions:

1. Prepare the Chicken:
    - Pound the chicken breasts or thighs to an even thickness. This helps them cook more evenly.

- In a shallow dish, pour the buttermilk over the chicken pieces, ensuring they are fully submerged. Let them marinate for at least 30 minutes, or up to overnight in the refrigerator.
- In another shallow dish, whisk together the flour, salt, pepper, paprika, and garlic powder.
- Remove the chicken from the buttermilk and dredge each piece in the flour mixture, shaking off any excess.

2. Fry the Chicken:
    - In a large skillet or deep fryer, heat the vegetable oil to 350°F (175°C).
    - Carefully place the chicken pieces in the hot oil, working in batches if necessary to avoid overcrowding the pan.
    - Fry the chicken for about 6-8 minutes per side, or until golden brown and cooked through. The internal temperature should reach 165°F (75°C). Remove the chicken from the oil and place it on a wire rack or paper towels to drain excess oil.

3. Make the Waffles:
    - Preheat your waffle iron according to the manufacturer's instructions.
    - In a large mixing bowl, whisk together the flour, baking powder, sugar, and salt.
    - In another bowl, beat the eggs and then stir in the milk and melted butter.
    - Pour the wet ingredients into the dry ingredients and stir until just combined. Do not overmix; it's okay if there are a few lumps.
    - Grease the waffle iron with vegetable oil or non-stick cooking spray. Pour the batter onto the preheated waffle iron and cook according to the manufacturer's instructions, until golden brown and crispy.

4. Serve:
    - Serve the fried chicken on top of the freshly cooked waffles.
    - Top with butter and drizzle with maple syrup.
    - Enjoy your delicious chicken and waffles!

This dish is perfect for breakfast, brunch, or even dinner. The combination of savory fried chicken and sweet, fluffy waffles is sure to be a hit with family and friends.

Hush puppies

Ingredients:

- 1 cup yellow cornmeal
- 1/2 cup all-purpose flour
- 1 teaspoon baking powder
- 1/2 teaspoon baking soda
- 1/2 teaspoon salt
- 1/4 teaspoon black pepper
- 1/2 cup finely chopped onion
- 1/4 cup finely chopped green bell pepper
- 1/4 cup finely chopped celery
- 1 large egg, beaten
- 1/2 cup buttermilk
- Vegetable oil, for frying

Instructions:

1. Prepare the Batter:
    - In a large mixing bowl, whisk together the cornmeal, flour, baking powder, baking soda, salt, and black pepper until well combined.
    - Stir in the chopped onion, green bell pepper, and celery until evenly distributed throughout the dry ingredients.
2. Make the Batter:
    - In a separate bowl, whisk together the beaten egg and buttermilk until smooth.
    - Pour the wet ingredients into the dry ingredients and stir until just combined. The batter should be thick and slightly lumpy.
3. Fry the Hush Puppies:
    - In a deep skillet or Dutch oven, heat about 2 inches of vegetable oil to 350°F (175°C) over medium heat.
    - Using a spoon or small ice cream scoop, drop spoonfuls of the batter into the hot oil, working in batches to avoid overcrowding the pan.
    - Fry the hush puppies for 2-3 minutes per side, or until golden brown and crispy, turning them halfway through cooking.
    - Use a slotted spoon to transfer the cooked hush puppies to a plate lined with paper towels to drain excess oil. Repeat with the remaining batter.

4. Serve:
    - Serve the hush puppies hot as a side dish or appetizer.
    - Enjoy them on their own or with a dipping sauce such as remoulade, tartar sauce, or honey butter.

These hush puppies are crispy on the outside, tender on the inside, and bursting with flavor from the onions, bell peppers, and celery. They're the perfect accompaniment to fried fish, shrimp, or barbecue, and they're sure to be a hit at any Southern-inspired meal or gathering.

Shrimp po'boy sandwich

Ingredients:

For the shrimp:

- 1 pound large shrimp, peeled and deveined
- 1 cup all-purpose flour
- 1 teaspoon salt
- 1/2 teaspoon black pepper
- 1/2 teaspoon paprika
- 1/2 teaspoon garlic powder
- Vegetable oil, for frying

For the remoulade sauce:

- 1/2 cup mayonnaise
- 2 tablespoons Creole mustard or whole grain mustard
- 1 tablespoon prepared horseradish
- 1 tablespoon lemon juice
- 1 teaspoon hot sauce (optional)
- 1 clove garlic, minced
- 1 tablespoon chopped fresh parsley
- Salt and black pepper to taste

For assembling:

- Baguette or French bread, cut into sandwich-sized pieces
- Lettuce leaves
- Sliced tomatoes
- Sliced pickles

Instructions:

1. Prepare the Remoulade Sauce:
    - In a small bowl, whisk together the mayonnaise, Creole mustard, horseradish, lemon juice, hot sauce (if using), minced garlic, chopped

parsley, salt, and black pepper until smooth and well combined. Taste and adjust seasoning as needed. Refrigerate until ready to use.
2. Bread and Fry the Shrimp:
   - In a shallow dish, combine the flour, salt, pepper, paprika, and garlic powder.
   - Heat vegetable oil in a deep skillet or Dutch oven over medium-high heat until it reaches 350°F (175°C).
   - Dredge the peeled and deveined shrimp in the seasoned flour mixture, shaking off any excess.
   - Carefully place the coated shrimp in the hot oil, working in batches if necessary to avoid overcrowding the pan.
   - Fry the shrimp for about 2-3 minutes per side, or until golden brown and crispy. Remove them from the oil using a slotted spoon and transfer them to a plate lined with paper towels to drain excess oil.
3. Assemble the Po'boy Sandwiches:
   - Split the baguette or French bread pieces in half horizontally, leaving a hinge on one side.
   - Spread a generous amount of remoulade sauce on the bottom half of each piece of bread.
   - Arrange lettuce leaves, sliced tomatoes, and sliced pickles on top of the remoulade sauce.
   - Place the fried shrimp on top of the vegetables, then close the sandwich with the top half of the bread.
   - Repeat with the remaining bread and shrimp to make additional sandwiches.
4. Serve:
   - Serve the Shrimp Po'boy sandwiches immediately, and enjoy the crispy shrimp and creamy remoulade sauce nestled in the soft bread with crisp, cool toppings.

These Shrimp Po'boy sandwiches are perfect for a casual lunch or dinner, and they're sure to be a hit with seafood lovers and fans of Southern cuisine alike.

Collard greens

Ingredients:

- 2 bunches of collard greens (about 2 pounds)
- 6 slices of bacon, chopped
- 1 onion, chopped
- 3 cloves of garlic, minced
- 4 cups chicken or vegetable broth
- 1 tablespoon apple cider vinegar
- 1 teaspoon sugar
- Salt and black pepper to taste
- Hot sauce (optional, for serving)

Instructions:

1. Prepare the Collard Greens:
   - Rinse the collard greens under cold water to remove any dirt or debris. Trim the tough stems from the leaves, then stack the leaves and cut them into thin strips.
2. Cook the Bacon and Onions:
   - In a large pot or Dutch oven, cook the chopped bacon over medium heat until it's browned and crispy. Remove the bacon from the pot and set it aside, leaving the rendered bacon fat in the pot.
   - Add the chopped onion to the pot and cook until it's softened and translucent, about 5 minutes. Add the minced garlic and cook for an additional 1-2 minutes.
3. Add the Collard Greens:
   - Add the collard greens to the pot in batches, stirring to wilt them down. Once all the collard greens are added, cook them for about 5 minutes, stirring occasionally, until they start to wilt.
4. Simmer the Collard Greens:
   - Pour the chicken or vegetable broth into the pot with the collard greens. Bring the liquid to a simmer, then reduce the heat to low. Cover the pot and let the collard greens simmer for 1-2 hours, stirring occasionally, until they are tender.
   - Add the cooked bacon back to the pot, along with the apple cider vinegar and sugar. Season with salt and black pepper to taste.

5. Serve:
    - Serve the collard greens hot, with a splash of hot sauce if desired.
    - Enjoy these flavorful and tender collard greens as a side dish with your favorite Southern meal.

This classic recipe for collard greens is a delicious and comforting way to enjoy this nutritious leafy green vegetable. Adjust the seasoning and add more or less broth according to your taste preferences.

Gumbo

Ingredients:

- 1/2 cup vegetable oil
- 1/2 cup all-purpose flour
- 1 onion, diced
- 1 bell pepper, diced
- 2 celery stalks, diced
- 3 cloves garlic, minced
- 1 pound andouille sausage, sliced
- 1 pound boneless, skinless chicken thighs, cut into bite-sized pieces
- 6 cups chicken broth
- 1 can (14.5 ounces) diced tomatoes
- 2 bay leaves
- 1 teaspoon dried thyme
- 1 teaspoon dried oregano
- 1/2 teaspoon cayenne pepper (optional, for heat)
- Salt and black pepper to taste
- 2 cups sliced okra (fresh or frozen)
- Cooked rice, for serving
- Chopped green onions, for garnish
- File powder (optional, for serving)

Instructions:

1. Make the Roux:
    - In a large Dutch oven or heavy-bottomed pot, heat the vegetable oil over medium heat. Gradually whisk in the flour, stirring constantly to combine.
    - Cook the roux, stirring frequently, until it turns a deep caramel color, similar to the color of peanut butter. This can take about 30-40 minutes. Be careful not to burn the roux, as it will impart a bitter flavor.
2. Sauté the Vegetables and Meat:
    - Once the roux is darkened, add the diced onion, bell pepper, celery, and minced garlic to the pot. Cook, stirring occasionally, until the vegetables are softened.
    - Add the sliced andouille sausage and diced chicken thighs to the pot. Cook, stirring occasionally, until the sausage is browned and the chicken is cooked through.

3. Add the Broth and Seasonings:
   - Pour in the chicken broth and diced tomatoes (with their juices) to the pot, stirring to combine.
   - Add the bay leaves, dried thyme, dried oregano, cayenne pepper (if using), salt, and black pepper to the pot. Stir to combine.
4. Simmer the Gumbo:
   - Bring the gumbo to a boil, then reduce the heat to low and let it simmer, uncovered, for about 1 hour, stirring occasionally.
   - Add the sliced okra to the pot and continue to simmer for an additional 30 minutes, or until the gumbo has thickened slightly and the flavors have melded together.
5. Serve:
   - Remove the bay leaves from the gumbo and discard them.
   - Serve the gumbo hot over cooked rice, garnished with chopped green onions.
   - Optionally, sprinkle file powder over each serving of gumbo just before serving, if desired.

Enjoy this flavorful and comforting chicken and sausage gumbo as a main dish for a taste of Louisiana cuisine! Adjust the seasonings and spices according to your taste preferences.

Fried green tomatoes

Ingredients:

- 4 large green tomatoes, sliced into 1/4-inch rounds
- 1 cup cornmeal or all-purpose flour
- 1 teaspoon salt
- 1/2 teaspoon black pepper
- 1/2 teaspoon paprika
- 1/4 teaspoon cayenne pepper (optional, for heat)
- 2 large eggs
- 2 tablespoons milk or buttermilk
- Vegetable oil, for frying
- Salt, for sprinkling (optional)

Instructions:

1. Prepare the Tomatoes:
    - Rinse the green tomatoes under cold water and pat them dry with paper towels. Slice them into 1/4-inch thick rounds, discarding the ends.
2. Season the Coating:
    - In a shallow dish, mix together the cornmeal or flour, salt, black pepper, paprika, and cayenne pepper (if using).
3. Prepare the Egg Wash:
    - In another shallow dish, whisk together the eggs and milk or buttermilk until well combined.
4. Coat the Tomatoes:
    - Dip each tomato slice into the egg wash, shaking off any excess.
    - Dredge the tomato slice in the seasoned cornmeal or flour mixture, coating it evenly on both sides. Press gently to adhere the coating.
5. Fry the Tomatoes:
    - In a large skillet or frying pan, heat about 1/4 inch of vegetable oil over medium heat until it reaches 350°F (175°C).
    - Carefully place the coated tomato slices in the hot oil, working in batches if necessary to avoid overcrowding the pan.
    - Fry the tomatoes for 2-3 minutes per side, or until they are golden brown and crispy. Use a spatula to carefully flip them halfway through cooking.
6. Drain and Serve:

- Once the tomatoes are fried to perfection, remove them from the oil and transfer them to a plate lined with paper towels to drain excess oil.
- Optionally, sprinkle the fried green tomatoes with a little extra salt while they are still hot.

7. Serve:
    - Serve the fried green tomatoes hot as a side dish or appetizer. They pair well with a variety of dipping sauces, such as remoulade, ranch dressing, or sriracha mayo.

Enjoy the crispy, tangy goodness of these Southern-style fried green tomatoes as a delicious addition to your meal!

Pimento cheese

Ingredients:

- 2 cups sharp cheddar cheese, shredded
- 1/2 cup mayonnaise
- 1/4 cup diced pimentos, drained
- 1 tablespoon finely grated onion (optional)
- 1 teaspoon Worcestershire sauce
- 1/4 teaspoon garlic powder
- 1/4 teaspoon paprika
- Salt and black pepper to taste
- Hot sauce (optional, for heat)

Instructions:

1. Mix the Ingredients:
    - In a mixing bowl, combine the shredded sharp cheddar cheese, mayonnaise, diced pimentos, finely grated onion (if using), Worcestershire sauce, garlic powder, paprika, salt, and black pepper.
    - If desired, add a few dashes of hot sauce for extra heat.
2. Stir Until Combined:
    - Stir the ingredients together until they are well combined and the cheese is evenly coated with the mayonnaise mixture.
3. Adjust Seasonings:
    - Taste the pimento cheese and adjust the seasonings as needed. Add more salt, pepper, or other seasonings to suit your taste preferences.
4. Chill (Optional):
    - For best flavor, cover the pimento cheese and refrigerate it for at least 1 hour before serving. This allows the flavors to meld together.
5. Serve:
    - Serve the pimento cheese as a spread for crackers, bread, or sandwiches.
    - Enjoy it as a delicious appetizer, snack, or party dip.

Pimento cheese is versatile and can be customized to your liking. Feel free to experiment with different types of cheese, additional seasonings, or mix-ins like diced jalapeños or chopped bacon. This classic Southern spread is sure to be a hit at any gathering!

Red beans and rice

Ingredients:

- 1 pound dried red kidney beans
- 1 pound smoked sausage or andouille sausage, sliced
- 1 onion, diced
- 1 bell pepper, diced
- 2 celery stalks, diced
- 3 cloves garlic, minced
- 2 bay leaves
- 1 teaspoon dried thyme
- 1 teaspoon dried oregano
- 1/2 teaspoon cayenne pepper (optional, for heat)
- Salt and black pepper to taste
- 6 cups chicken broth or water
- Cooked white rice, for serving
- Chopped green onions, for garnish

Instructions:

1. Prepare the Beans:
    - Rinse the dried red kidney beans under cold water and pick out any debris or shriveled beans. Soak the beans overnight in a large bowl of water, or use the quick soak method by bringing them to a boil in a pot of water, removing from heat, and letting them soak for 1 hour.
2. Sauté the Sausage and Vegetables:
    - In a large pot or Dutch oven, cook the sliced sausage over medium heat until browned and cooked through. Remove the sausage from the pot and set it aside, leaving the rendered fat in the pot.
    - Add the diced onion, bell pepper, celery, and minced garlic to the pot. Cook, stirring occasionally, until the vegetables are softened.
3. Simmer the Beans:
    - Drain the soaked beans and add them to the pot with the sautéed vegetables. Pour in the chicken broth or water to cover the beans by about 2 inches.
    - Add the bay leaves, dried thyme, dried oregano, cayenne pepper (if using), salt, and black pepper to the pot. Stir to combine.

- Bring the mixture to a boil, then reduce the heat to low and let it simmer, partially covered, for about 1.5 to 2 hours, or until the beans are tender and the liquid has thickened to your desired consistency. Stir occasionally and add more broth or water if needed to prevent the beans from sticking to the bottom of the pot.
4. Mash Some Beans (Optional):
    - For a creamier texture, use the back of a spoon or a potato masher to mash some of the beans against the side of the pot. This will help thicken the sauce.
5. Finish and Serve:
    - Return the cooked sausage to the pot and stir to combine. Taste and adjust the seasoning as needed.
    - Serve the red beans and sausage hot over cooked white rice.
    - Garnish with chopped green onions before serving.

Red beans and rice is a comforting and satisfying dish that's perfect for a cozy meal any time of year. Enjoy the rich flavors of this classic Southern favorite!

Buttermilk pie

Ingredients:

For the pie crust:

- 1 1/4 cups all-purpose flour
- 1/2 teaspoon salt
- 1/2 cup unsalted butter, cold and cubed
- 3-4 tablespoons ice water

For the filling:

- 1 1/2 cups granulated sugar
- 1/4 cup all-purpose flour
- 1/2 cup unsalted butter, melted and cooled slightly
- 3 large eggs
- 1 cup buttermilk
- 1 tablespoon vanilla extract
- 1 tablespoon lemon juice
- 1/4 teaspoon ground nutmeg
- 1/4 teaspoon salt

Instructions:

1. Prepare the Pie Crust:
    - In a large mixing bowl, combine the flour and salt. Add the cold, cubed butter to the flour mixture.
    - Use a pastry cutter or your fingertips to work the butter into the flour until the mixture resembles coarse crumbs.
    - Gradually add the ice water, 1 tablespoon at a time, and mix until the dough comes together. Be careful not to overwork the dough.
    - Shape the dough into a disk, wrap it in plastic wrap, and refrigerate it for at least 30 minutes.
2. Preheat the Oven:
    - Preheat your oven to 350°F (175°C).
3. Roll Out the Dough:

- On a lightly floured surface, roll out the chilled pie dough into a circle about 12 inches in diameter. Carefully transfer the dough to a 9-inch pie dish and press it gently into the bottom and sides. Trim any excess dough and crimp the edges as desired.
4. Prepare the Filling:
    - In a large mixing bowl, whisk together the granulated sugar and flour until well combined.
    - Add the melted butter and whisk until smooth.
    - Beat in the eggs, one at a time, until fully incorporated.
    - Stir in the buttermilk, vanilla extract, lemon juice, nutmeg, and salt until the filling is smooth and well combined.
5. Bake the Pie:
    - Pour the filling into the prepared pie crust.
    - Place the pie on a baking sheet and bake in the preheated oven for 45-50 minutes, or until the filling is set and the top is golden brown.
    - If the crust starts to brown too quickly, cover the edges with aluminum foil or a pie crust shield to prevent burning.
6. Cool and Serve:
    - Allow the buttermilk pie to cool completely on a wire rack before slicing and serving.
    - Serve slices of buttermilk pie at room temperature or chilled, with a dollop of whipped cream or a sprinkle of powdered sugar, if desired.

Enjoy this delicious and comforting Southern dessert with its creamy, tangy filling and buttery crust!

Cornbread

Ingredients:

- 1 cup yellow cornmeal
- 1 cup all-purpose flour
- 1/4 cup granulated sugar (optional, for sweeter cornbread)
- 1 tablespoon baking powder
- 1 teaspoon salt
- 1 cup buttermilk
- 1/2 cup unsalted butter, melted and cooled slightly
- 2 large eggs

Instructions:

1. Preheat the Oven:
    - Preheat your oven to 400°F (200°C). Grease a 9-inch square baking dish or cast iron skillet.
2. Mix the Dry Ingredients:
    - In a large mixing bowl, whisk together the yellow cornmeal, all-purpose flour, sugar (if using), baking powder, and salt until well combined.
3. Combine Wet Ingredients:
    - In a separate bowl, whisk together the buttermilk, melted butter, and eggs until smooth.
4. Mix Wet and Dry Ingredients:
    - Pour the wet ingredients into the bowl with the dry ingredients. Stir until just combined. Do not overmix; a few lumps are okay.
5. Bake the Cornbread:
    - Pour the batter into the prepared baking dish or skillet, spreading it evenly.
    - Bake in the preheated oven for 20-25 minutes, or until the cornbread is golden brown on top and a toothpick inserted into the center comes out clean.
6. Cool and Serve:
    - Allow the cornbread to cool in the pan for a few minutes before slicing and serving.
    - Serve the cornbread warm, with butter and honey, if desired.

This classic cornbread recipe is perfect for serving alongside barbecue, chili, or Southern comfort food dishes. Feel free to customize it by adding ingredients like chopped jalapeños, shredded cheese, or cooked bacon for extra flavor!

Sweet tea

Ingredients:

- 4 cups water
- 4 black tea bags
- 1/2 - 3/4 cup granulated sugar (adjust to taste)
- Ice cubes
- Lemon slices (optional, for garnish)
- Fresh mint leaves (optional, for garnish)

Instructions:

1. Boil Water:
   - In a medium saucepan, bring 4 cups of water to a boil.
2. Steep Tea Bags:
   - Once the water is boiling, remove it from the heat. Add the black tea bags to the hot water and let them steep for 5-10 minutes, depending on how strong you prefer your tea.
3. Sweeten Tea:
   - Remove the tea bags from the water and discard them. Stir in the granulated sugar while the tea is still hot, adjusting the amount to your desired level of sweetness. Stir until the sugar is completely dissolved.
4. Chill Tea:
   - Transfer the sweetened tea to a heatproof pitcher and let it cool to room temperature.
5. Serve:
   - Once the tea has cooled, refrigerate it until chilled, about 1-2 hours.
   - To serve, fill glasses with ice cubes and pour the chilled sweet tea over the ice.
   - Garnish each glass with a lemon slice and a sprig of fresh mint, if desired.
   - Stir the sweet tea before serving to distribute the sweetness evenly.

Enjoy this refreshing and classic Southern sweet tea on a hot day or any time you need a thirst-quenching beverage! Adjust the sweetness and add lemon or mint according to your taste preferences.

Pulled pork barbecue

Ingredients:

For the pork:

- 4-5 pounds pork shoulder or pork butt (bone-in or boneless)
- 2 tablespoons brown sugar
- 2 tablespoons paprika
- 1 tablespoon garlic powder
- 1 tablespoon onion powder
- 1 tablespoon ground cumin
- 1 tablespoon chili powder
- 1 tablespoon salt
- 1 teaspoon black pepper
- 1/2 teaspoon cayenne pepper (optional, for heat)
- 1 cup chicken broth or water
- 1/2 cup apple cider vinegar
- Barbecue sauce (optional, for serving)

For serving:

- Hamburger buns or sandwich rolls
- Coleslaw (optional, for topping)

Instructions:

1. Prepare the Pork:
    - In a small bowl, mix together the brown sugar, paprika, garlic powder, onion powder, cumin, chili powder, salt, black pepper, and cayenne pepper (if using) to make the dry rub.
    - Rub the dry rub all over the pork shoulder or pork butt, ensuring that it's evenly coated. Let the seasoned pork sit at room temperature for about 30 minutes to allow the flavors to penetrate.
2. Preheat the Oven (or Prepare the Smoker):
    - Preheat your oven to 300°F (150°C). Alternatively, you can cook the pork on a smoker preheated to 250°F (120°C) for added flavor.

3. Cook the Pork:
   - Place the seasoned pork in a roasting pan or on a rack set inside a baking dish. Pour the chicken broth or water and apple cider vinegar into the bottom of the pan.
   - Cover the pan tightly with aluminum foil and transfer it to the preheated oven. Alternatively, place the pork in the smoker.
   - Cook the pork for 5-6 hours, or until it's tender and easily pulls apart with a fork. If using a smoker, maintain a temperature of 250°F (120°C) and smoke the pork for 8-10 hours, or until it reaches an internal temperature of 195-205°F (90-96°C).
4. Shred the Pork:
   - Once the pork is cooked, remove it from the oven or smoker and let it rest for 10-15 minutes. Use two forks to shred the meat into bite-sized pieces, discarding any excess fat or bones.
5. Serve:
   - Serve the pulled pork barbecue on hamburger buns or sandwich rolls, topped with barbecue sauce and coleslaw if desired.
   - Enjoy this classic Southern dish as a main course for a backyard barbecue or casual gathering!

Pulled pork barbecue is delicious on its own, but serving it on a sandwich with coleslaw adds extra flavor and texture. Adjust the seasonings and cooking time according to your preferences and equipment.

Fried catfish

Ingredients:

For the pork:

- 4-5 pounds pork shoulder or pork butt (bone-in or boneless)
- 2 tablespoons brown sugar
- 2 tablespoons paprika
- 1 tablespoon garlic powder
- 1 tablespoon onion powder
- 1 tablespoon ground cumin
- 1 tablespoon chili powder
- 1 tablespoon salt
- 1 teaspoon black pepper
- 1/2 teaspoon cayenne pepper (optional, for heat)
- 1 cup chicken broth or water
- 1/2 cup apple cider vinegar
- Barbecue sauce (optional, for serving)

For serving:

- Hamburger buns or sandwich rolls
- Coleslaw (optional, for topping)

Instructions:

1. Prepare the Pork:
    - In a small bowl, mix together the brown sugar, paprika, garlic powder, onion powder, cumin, chili powder, salt, black pepper, and cayenne pepper (if using) to make the dry rub.
    - Rub the dry rub all over the pork shoulder or pork butt, ensuring that it's evenly coated. Let the seasoned pork sit at room temperature for about 30 minutes to allow the flavors to penetrate.
2. Preheat the Oven (or Prepare the Smoker):
    - Preheat your oven to 300°F (150°C). Alternatively, you can cook the pork on a smoker preheated to 250°F (120°C) for added flavor.

3. Cook the Pork:
   - Place the seasoned pork in a roasting pan or on a rack set inside a baking dish. Pour the chicken broth or water and apple cider vinegar into the bottom of the pan.
   - Cover the pan tightly with aluminum foil and transfer it to the preheated oven. Alternatively, place the pork in the smoker.
   - Cook the pork for 5-6 hours, or until it's tender and easily pulls apart with a fork. If using a smoker, maintain a temperature of 250°F (120°C) and smoke the pork for 8-10 hours, or until it reaches an internal temperature of 195-205°F (90-96°C).
4. Shred the Pork:
   - Once the pork is cooked, remove it from the oven or smoker and let it rest for 10-15 minutes. Use two forks to shred the meat into bite-sized pieces, discarding any excess fat or bones.
5. Serve:
   - Serve the pulled pork barbecue on hamburger buns or sandwich rolls, topped with barbecue sauce and coleslaw if desired.
   - Enjoy this classic Southern dish as a main course for a backyard barbecue or casual gathering!

Pulled pork barbecue is delicious on its own, but serving it on a sandwich with coleslaw adds extra flavor and texture. Adjust the seasonings and cooking time according to your preferences and equipment.

Fried catfish

Fried catfish is a classic Southern dish known for its crispy coating and tender, flavorful fish. Here's a simple recipe to make it at home:

Ingredients:

- 4 catfish fillets (about 6-8 ounces each)
- 1 cup cornmeal
- 1/2 cup all-purpose flour
- 1 teaspoon salt
- 1/2 teaspoon black pepper
- 1/2 teaspoon garlic powder
- 1/2 teaspoon paprika
- Vegetable oil, for frying
- Lemon wedges, for serving
- Tartar sauce, for serving

Instructions:

1. Prepare the Catfish:
    - Rinse the catfish fillets under cold water and pat them dry with paper towels. Cut the fillets into smaller pieces if desired.
2. Mix the Coating:
    - In a shallow dish or pie plate, combine the cornmeal, all-purpose flour, salt, black pepper, garlic powder, and paprika. Stir until well combined.
3. Coat the Catfish:
    - Dredge each catfish fillet in the cornmeal mixture, pressing gently to adhere the coating to both sides of the fish. Shake off any excess coating.
4. Heat the Oil:
    - In a large skillet or frying pan, heat about 1/2 inch of vegetable oil over medium-high heat until it reaches 350°F (175°C). You can also use a deep fryer if you have one.
5. Fry the Catfish:
    - Carefully place the coated catfish fillets in the hot oil, working in batches if necessary to avoid overcrowding the pan.

- Fry the catfish for 3-4 minutes per side, or until the coating is golden brown and crispy and the fish is cooked through. Use a spatula to carefully flip the fillets halfway through cooking.
6. Drain and Serve:
    - Once the catfish is cooked to perfection, use a slotted spoon or spatula to transfer it to a plate lined with paper towels to drain excess oil.
    - Serve the fried catfish hot, with lemon wedges and tartar sauce on the side for dipping.

Enjoy this delicious fried catfish as a main course for a Southern-inspired meal. Pair it with hush puppies, coleslaw, and collard greens for a complete and satisfying dinner!

Cajun shrimp boil

Ingredients:

- 2 pounds large shrimp, unpeeled
- 1 pound smoked sausage or andouille sausage, sliced into chunks
- 4 ears of corn, shucked and cut into thirds
- 1 pound small red potatoes, halved or quartered
- 2 lemons, halved
- 4 cloves garlic, smashed
- 2 bay leaves
- 2 tablespoons Old Bay seasoning
- 2 tablespoons Cajun seasoning
- 1 tablespoon whole black peppercorns
- 1 tablespoon salt
- Water

Instructions:

1. Prepare the Pot:
    - Fill a large stockpot or Dutch oven halfway with water. Add the halved lemons, smashed garlic cloves, bay leaves, Old Bay seasoning, Cajun seasoning, whole black peppercorns, and salt to the pot.
2. Bring to a Boil:
    - Place the pot over high heat and bring the seasoned water to a rolling boil.
3. Add the Ingredients:
    - Once the water is boiling, add the sausage slices, halved potatoes, and corn pieces to the pot. Let them cook for about 10 minutes, partially covered, until they are just beginning to soften.
4. Add the Shrimp:
    - Add the unpeeled shrimp to the pot and continue to cook for an additional 3-5 minutes, or until the shrimp are pink and opaque.
5. Drain and Serve:
    - Once the shrimp are cooked through, turn off the heat. Use a slotted spoon to transfer the shrimp, sausage, potatoes, and corn to a large serving platter or directly onto a newspaper-lined table.
    - Serve the Cajun shrimp boil hot, with additional lemon wedges and Cajun seasoning for seasoning to taste.

6. Enjoy:
    - To eat, simply peel the shrimp and enjoy the flavorful combination of shrimp, sausage, corn, and potatoes.

Cajun shrimp boil is a fun and delicious dish that's perfect for serving at casual gatherings or backyard cookouts. Customize it with your favorite seafood, sausage, and vegetables, and adjust the seasoning to suit your taste preferences.

Peach cobbler

Ingredients:

For the filling:

- 6 cups fresh or canned peaches, sliced (about 6-8 peaches)
- 1 cup granulated sugar
- 2 tablespoons all-purpose flour
- 1 teaspoon ground cinnamon
- 1/4 teaspoon ground nutmeg
- 1 tablespoon lemon juice

For the crust:

- 1 1/2 cups all-purpose flour
- 1/2 cup granulated sugar
- 1 teaspoon baking powder
- 1/2 teaspoon salt
- 1/2 cup unsalted butter, cold and cubed
- 1/4 cup boiling water

For serving:

- Vanilla ice cream or whipped cream (optional)

Instructions:

1. Preheat the Oven:
    - Preheat your oven to 375°F (190°C).
2. Prepare the Peach Filling:
    - In a large mixing bowl, combine the sliced peaches, granulated sugar, all-purpose flour, ground cinnamon, ground nutmeg, and lemon juice. Toss until the peaches are evenly coated in the sugar and spices. Set aside.
3. Make the Crust:
    - In a separate mixing bowl, whisk together the all-purpose flour, granulated sugar, baking powder, and salt.

- Cut in the cold, cubed butter using a pastry cutter or your fingertips, until the mixture resembles coarse crumbs.
- Gradually add the boiling water to the flour mixture, stirring until a soft dough forms. Set aside.

4. Assemble the Cobbler:
    - Transfer the peach filling to a 9x13-inch baking dish or a similar-sized casserole dish, spreading it out evenly.
    - Drop spoonfuls of the biscuit dough over the top of the peach filling, covering it as evenly as possible.
5. Bake the Cobbler:
    - Place the baking dish in the preheated oven and bake for 40-45 minutes, or until the crust is golden brown and the peach filling is bubbly around the edges.
6. Serve:
    - Remove the peach cobbler from the oven and let it cool for a few minutes before serving.
    - Serve warm, topped with vanilla ice cream or whipped cream if desired.

Enjoy this delicious and comforting peach cobbler as a delightful dessert, perfect for summer gatherings or cozy evenings at home!

Biscuits with sausage gravy

Ingredients:

For the biscuits:

- 2 cups all-purpose flour
- 1 tablespoon baking powder
- 1 teaspoon salt
- 1/2 cup unsalted butter, cold and cubed
- 3/4 cup milk

For the sausage gravy:

- 1/2 pound breakfast sausage (pork or turkey)
- 1/4 cup all-purpose flour
- 2 cups milk
- Salt and black pepper to taste
- Optional: pinch of cayenne pepper or paprika for heat

Instructions:

1. Make the Biscuits:
    - Preheat your oven to 425°F (220°C).
    - In a large mixing bowl, whisk together the flour, baking powder, and salt.
    - Add the cold, cubed butter to the flour mixture. Use a pastry cutter or your fingertips to work the butter into the flour until the mixture resembles coarse crumbs.
    - Gradually add the milk to the flour mixture, stirring until a soft dough forms.
    - Turn the dough out onto a lightly floured surface and gently knead it a few times until it comes together.
    - Roll out the dough to about 1/2 inch thickness. Use a biscuit cutter or the rim of a glass to cut out biscuits.
    - Place the biscuits on a baking sheet lined with parchment paper, leaving a little space between each biscuit.
    - Bake in the preheated oven for 12-15 minutes, or until the biscuits are golden brown and cooked through.
2. Make the Sausage Gravy:

- While the biscuits are baking, cook the breakfast sausage in a skillet over medium heat, breaking it up into small pieces with a spoon, until it's browned and cooked through.
- Sprinkle the cooked sausage with flour, stirring to coat the sausage evenly. Cook for 1-2 minutes to cook out the raw flour taste.
- Gradually pour in the milk, stirring constantly to prevent lumps from forming. Bring the gravy to a simmer and cook until it thickens to your desired consistency, about 5-7 minutes.
- Season the gravy with salt, black pepper, and a pinch of cayenne pepper or paprika for heat, if desired. Adjust seasoning to taste.

3. Serve:
    - Split the warm biscuits in half and place them on serving plates.
    - Ladle the hot sausage gravy over the biscuits.
    - Serve immediately and enjoy!

Biscuits with sausage gravy are a comforting and satisfying breakfast treat, perfect for weekend brunches or special occasions. Adjust the seasoning and thickness of the gravy according to your preferences.

Crawfish étouffée

Ingredients:

- 1/2 cup unsalted butter
- 1/2 cup all-purpose flour
- 1 large onion, diced
- 1 bell pepper, diced
- 2 celery stalks, diced
- 4 cloves garlic, minced
- 2 cups seafood or chicken broth
- 1 pound cooked crawfish tails, peeled
- 1 tablespoon Creole seasoning (or to taste)
- 1 teaspoon paprika
- 1/2 teaspoon dried thyme
- 1/2 teaspoon dried oregano
- Salt and black pepper to taste
- 1/4 cup chopped green onions, for garnish
- Cooked white rice, for serving

Instructions:

1. Make the Roux:
    - In a large Dutch oven or heavy-bottomed pot, melt the butter over medium heat.
    - Gradually whisk in the flour to form a smooth paste. Continue cooking, stirring constantly, until the roux turns a deep golden brown color, similar to peanut butter. Be careful not to burn it.
2. Sauté the Vegetables:
    - Add the diced onion, bell pepper, celery, and minced garlic to the pot. Cook, stirring occasionally, until the vegetables are softened, about 5-7 minutes.
3. Add Broth and Seasonings:
    - Slowly pour in the seafood or chicken broth, stirring continuously to incorporate it into the roux.
    - Add the Creole seasoning, paprika, dried thyme, dried oregano, salt, and black pepper. Stir to combine.
4. Simmer:

- Bring the mixture to a simmer, then reduce the heat to low. Let it simmer uncovered for about 15-20 minutes, stirring occasionally, to allow the flavors to meld together and the sauce to thicken.

5. Add Crawfish Tails:
    - Stir in the cooked crawfish tails, making sure they are evenly coated with the sauce.
    - Continue to simmer for an additional 5-7 minutes, or until the crawfish tails are heated through.
6. Serve:
    - Serve the crawfish étouffée hot over cooked white rice.
    - Garnish with chopped green onions before serving.

Enjoy this delicious and comforting crawfish étouffée, a flavorful taste of Cajun cuisine! Adjust the seasoning according to your taste preferences, and feel free to add a dash of hot sauce for extra heat if desired.

Blackened fish

Ingredients:

- 4 fish fillets (such as redfish, trout, snapper, or catfish), about 6-8 ounces each
- 2 tablespoons paprika
- 1 tablespoon garlic powder
- 1 tablespoon onion powder
- 1 tablespoon dried thyme
- 1 tablespoon dried oregano
- 1 teaspoon cayenne pepper (adjust to taste)
- 1 teaspoon black pepper
- 1 teaspoon salt
- 1/2 cup unsalted butter, melted
- Lemon wedges, for serving
- Fresh chopped parsley, for garnish (optional)

Instructions:

1. Prepare the Spice Mixture:
    - In a small bowl, combine the paprika, garlic powder, onion powder, dried thyme, dried oregano, cayenne pepper, black pepper, and salt. Mix well to combine.
2. Preheat the Skillet:
    - Heat a cast iron skillet or heavy-bottomed skillet over high heat until it's smoking hot. Make sure your kitchen is well-ventilated as the spices may create some smoke.
3. Coat the Fish:
    - Brush both sides of each fish fillet with melted butter.
    - Sprinkle the spice mixture generously over both sides of each fillet, pressing gently to adhere the spices to the fish.
4. Cook the Fish:
    - Carefully place the seasoned fish fillets in the hot skillet. You may need to work in batches depending on the size of your skillet.
    - Cook the fish for 2-3 minutes on each side, or until the spices are blackened and the fish is cooked through. The fish should easily flake with a fork when done.
5. Serve:
    - Transfer the blackened fish fillets to a serving platter.

- Serve hot with lemon wedges on the side for squeezing over the fish.
- Garnish with fresh chopped parsley if desired.

Enjoy this delicious and spicy blackened fish as a main course, served with your favorite side dishes such as rice, steamed vegetables, or a fresh salad. Adjust the level of cayenne pepper according to your taste preferences for more or less heat.

Southern-style macaroni and cheese

Ingredients:

- 1 pound elbow macaroni
- 1/2 cup unsalted butter
- 1/2 cup all-purpose flour
- 4 cups whole milk
- 2 cups shredded sharp cheddar cheese
- 1 cup shredded mozzarella cheese
- 1 cup shredded Monterey Jack cheese
- 1/2 teaspoon garlic powder
- 1/2 teaspoon onion powder
- 1/4 teaspoon cayenne pepper (optional)
- Salt and black pepper to taste
- 1 cup breadcrumbs (optional, for topping)
- Chopped fresh parsley, for garnish (optional)

Instructions:

1. Cook the Macaroni:
    - Bring a large pot of salted water to a boil. Cook the elbow macaroni according to the package instructions until al dente. Drain and set aside.
2. Make the Cheese Sauce:
    - In a large saucepan or Dutch oven, melt the butter over medium heat.
    - Stir in the all-purpose flour to make a roux. Cook, stirring constantly, for 1-2 minutes to cook out the raw flour taste.
    - Gradually whisk in the whole milk, stirring constantly to prevent lumps from forming.
    - Cook the sauce, stirring frequently, until it thickens and coats the back of a spoon, about 5-7 minutes.
    - Stir in the shredded cheddar cheese, shredded mozzarella cheese, and shredded Monterey Jack cheese until melted and smooth.
    - Season the cheese sauce with garlic powder, onion powder, cayenne pepper (if using), salt, and black pepper to taste. Adjust seasoning to your preference.
3. Combine Macaroni and Cheese Sauce:

- Add the cooked elbow macaroni to the cheese sauce, stirring until well combined and the macaroni is evenly coated with the cheese sauce.
4. Bake (Optional):
    - If desired, transfer the macaroni and cheese mixture to a greased baking dish. Sprinkle breadcrumbs over the top for a crunchy topping.
    - Bake in a preheated 350°F (175°C) oven for 20-25 minutes, or until the top is golden brown and bubbly.
5. Serve:
    - Remove the macaroni and cheese from the oven and let it cool for a few minutes.
    - Garnish with chopped fresh parsley if desired.
    - Serve hot as a comforting side dish or main course.

Enjoy this delicious and indulgent Southern-style macaroni and cheese, perfect for sharing with family and friends at any occasion!

Banana pudding

Ingredients:

- 3/4 cup granulated sugar
- 1/4 cup all-purpose flour
- 1/4 teaspoon salt
- 3 cups whole milk
- 4 large egg yolks
- 2 teaspoons vanilla extract
- 3 ripe bananas, sliced
- 1 (11 oz) box vanilla wafers
- Whipped cream or meringue for topping
- Additional banana slices and vanilla wafers for garnish (optional)

Instructions:

1. Prepare the Pudding:
    - In a medium saucepan, whisk together the granulated sugar, flour, and salt.
    - Gradually whisk in the milk until smooth.
    - Cook the mixture over medium heat, stirring constantly, until it thickens and comes to a gentle boil, about 8-10 minutes.
2. Temper the Eggs:
    - In a separate bowl, whisk the egg yolks until smooth.
    - Gradually whisk in about 1 cup of the hot milk mixture into the egg yolks to temper them, whisking constantly.
3. Combine and Cook:
    - Pour the tempered egg mixture back into the saucepan with the remaining hot milk mixture, whisking constantly.
    - Cook, stirring constantly, for an additional 2-3 minutes until the mixture thickens further.
    - Remove the saucepan from the heat and stir in the vanilla extract.
4. Assemble the Banana Pudding:
    - In a trifle dish or serving bowl, layer half of the sliced bananas on the bottom.
    - Top with a layer of vanilla wafers, breaking some of them in half if needed to fit.

- Pour half of the pudding mixture over the bananas and wafers, spreading it out evenly.
- Repeat the layers with the remaining bananas, wafers, and pudding.

5. Chill:
    - Cover the banana pudding with plastic wrap, pressing the wrap directly onto the surface of the pudding to prevent a skin from forming.
    - Refrigerate the banana pudding for at least 4 hours or overnight to chill and set.

6. Serve:
    - Before serving, top the chilled banana pudding with whipped cream or meringue.
    - Garnish with additional banana slices and vanilla wafers if desired.
    - Serve chilled and enjoy!

This creamy and delicious banana pudding is sure to be a hit at any gathering or potluck. Adjust the sweetness and thickness of the pudding to your preference, and feel free to get creative with the toppings and garnishes.

Chicken fried steak

Ingredients:

For the steak:

- 4 tenderized beef cube steaks (about 6-8 ounces each)
- Salt and black pepper to taste
- 1 cup all-purpose flour
- 1 teaspoon garlic powder
- 1 teaspoon paprika
- 1/2 teaspoon cayenne pepper (optional, for heat)
- 2 large eggs
- 1/4 cup milk
- Vegetable oil, for frying

For the gravy:

- 1/4 cup pan drippings (from frying the steak) or vegetable oil
- 1/4 cup all-purpose flour
- 2 cups whole milk or half-and-half
- Salt and black pepper to taste

Instructions:

1. Prepare the Steak:
    - Season both sides of the cube steaks with salt and black pepper.
    - In a shallow dish, combine the all-purpose flour, garlic powder, paprika, and cayenne pepper (if using).
    - In another shallow dish, whisk together the eggs and milk.
    - Dredge each steak in the flour mixture, shaking off any excess, then dip it into the egg mixture, and finally dredge it in the flour mixture again, pressing gently to adhere the coating. Repeat with the remaining steaks.
2. Fry the Steak:
    - Heat about 1/4 inch of vegetable oil in a large skillet over medium-high heat until hot but not smoking.
    - Carefully place the breaded steaks in the hot oil, working in batches if necessary to avoid overcrowding the skillet.

- Fry the steaks for 3-4 minutes on each side, or until golden brown and crispy. Use tongs to carefully flip the steaks halfway through cooking.

3. Make the Gravy:
    - Once all the steaks are cooked, remove them from the skillet and transfer them to a paper towel-lined plate to drain excess oil.
    - Pour off all but 1/4 cup of the pan drippings from the skillet (or add additional oil if needed).
    - Whisk in the all-purpose flour into the pan drippings to make a roux. Cook, stirring constantly, for 1-2 minutes to cook out the raw flour taste.
    - Gradually whisk in the whole milk or half-and-half, stirring constantly to prevent lumps from forming. Cook the gravy, stirring frequently, until thickened, about 5-7 minutes.
    - Season the gravy with salt and black pepper to taste.

4. Serve:
    - Serve the chicken fried steak hot, topped with the creamy gravy.
    - Serve with mashed potatoes, biscuits, or your favorite side dishes.

Enjoy this classic Southern comfort food dish with its crispy, golden exterior and tender, flavorful steak inside, smothered in creamy gravy!

Shrimp and okra gumbo

Ingredients:

- 1/2 cup vegetable oil
- 1/2 cup all-purpose flour
- 1 large onion, chopped
- 1 bell pepper, chopped
- 2 celery stalks, chopped
- 4 cloves garlic, minced
- 1 pound fresh or frozen okra, sliced
- 1 (14.5 oz) can diced tomatoes
- 6 cups seafood or chicken broth
- 1 pound shrimp, peeled and deveined
- 2 teaspoons Creole seasoning (or to taste)
- 1 teaspoon dried thyme
- 1 teaspoon dried oregano
- 1 bay leaf
- Salt and black pepper to taste
- Cooked white rice, for serving
- Chopped green onions, for garnish
- File powder (optional, for serving)

Instructions:

1. Make the Roux:
    - In a large Dutch oven or heavy-bottomed pot, heat the vegetable oil over medium heat. Gradually whisk in the all-purpose flour to make a roux.
    - Cook the roux, stirring constantly, until it turns a dark caramel color, similar to milk chocolate, about 20-30 minutes. Be careful not to burn the roux.
2. Sauté the Vegetables:
    - Add the chopped onion, bell pepper, and celery to the roux. Cook, stirring occasionally, until the vegetables are softened, about 5-7 minutes.
    - Stir in the minced garlic and cook for an additional 1-2 minutes until fragrant.
3. Add Okra and Tomatoes:
    - Add the sliced okra to the pot and cook for 5 minutes, stirring occasionally.

- Stir in the diced tomatoes (with their juices) and cook for another 5 minutes.
4. Simmer the Gumbo:
    - Pour in the seafood or chicken broth, stirring to combine. Add the Creole seasoning, dried thyme, dried oregano, and bay leaf.
    - Bring the gumbo to a boil, then reduce the heat to low and let it simmer, uncovered, for about 30 minutes to allow the flavors to meld together and the okra to soften.
5. Add Shrimp:
    - Stir in the peeled and deveined shrimp, cooking until they turn pink and opaque, about 5 minutes. Be careful not to overcook the shrimp.
6. Season and Serve:
    - Season the gumbo with salt and black pepper to taste.
    - Remove the bay leaf before serving.
    - Serve the shrimp and okra gumbo hot over cooked white rice.
    - Garnish with chopped green onions and sprinkle with file powder, if desired.

Enjoy this delicious and flavorful shrimp and okra gumbo as a comforting meal on its own or as part of a larger Creole feast! Adjust the seasoning and thickness of the gumbo according to your taste preferences.

Pecan pie

Ingredients:

For the pie crust:

- 1 1/4 cups all-purpose flour
- 1/2 teaspoon salt
- 1/2 cup unsalted butter, cold and cut into cubes
- 2-4 tablespoons ice water

For the filling:

- 1 cup granulated sugar
- 1 cup light corn syrup
- 3 large eggs
- 1 teaspoon vanilla extract
- 1/4 teaspoon salt
- 1 1/2 cups pecan halves

Instructions:

1. Prepare the Pie Crust:
    - In a large mixing bowl, whisk together the all-purpose flour and salt.
    - Add the cold, cubed butter to the flour mixture. Use a pastry cutter or your fingertips to work the butter into the flour until the mixture resembles coarse crumbs.
    - Gradually add the ice water, 1 tablespoon at a time, mixing with a fork until the dough comes together into a ball. Be careful not to overwork the dough.
    - Flatten the dough into a disk, wrap it in plastic wrap, and refrigerate it for at least 30 minutes.
2. Preheat the Oven:
    - Preheat your oven to 350°F (175°C).
3. Roll Out the Dough:
    - On a lightly floured surface, roll out the chilled dough into a circle large enough to fit into a 9-inch pie dish. Transfer the rolled-out dough to the pie

dish, pressing it gently into the bottom and sides. Trim any excess dough and crimp the edges as desired.
4. Prepare the Filling:
   - In a large mixing bowl, whisk together the granulated sugar, light corn syrup, eggs, vanilla extract, and salt until smooth.
   - Stir in the pecan halves until they are evenly coated in the mixture.
5. Assemble and Bake the Pie:
   - Pour the pecan filling into the prepared pie crust, spreading it out evenly.
   - Place the pie dish on a baking sheet to catch any drips, and transfer it to the preheated oven.
   - Bake the pecan pie for 50-60 minutes, or until the filling is set and the crust is golden brown. If the crust starts to brown too quickly, you can cover the edges with aluminum foil halfway through baking.
6. Cool and Serve:
   - Remove the pecan pie from the oven and let it cool completely on a wire rack before slicing and serving.
   - Serve the pecan pie at room temperature, optionally topped with whipped cream or vanilla ice cream.

Enjoy this classic pecan pie as a deliciously sweet ending to any meal, or as a special treat for holidays and celebrations!

Barbecue ribs

Ingredients:

For the ribs:

- 2 racks of pork baby back ribs (about 2-3 pounds each)
- Salt and black pepper to taste
- Your favorite barbecue rub or seasoning blend

For the barbecue sauce:

- 1 cup ketchup
- 1/2 cup apple cider vinegar
- 1/4 cup brown sugar
- 2 tablespoons Worcestershire sauce
- 1 tablespoon Dijon mustard
- 1 tablespoon smoked paprika
- 1 teaspoon garlic powder
- 1 teaspoon onion powder
- 1/2 teaspoon cayenne pepper (optional, for heat)
- Salt and black pepper to taste

Instructions:

1. Preheat the Oven:
    - Preheat your oven to 300°F (150°C).
2. Prepare the Ribs:
    - Remove the membrane from the back of the ribs: Use a butter knife to loosen one end of the membrane, then grip it with a paper towel and peel it off.
    - Season the ribs generously with salt, black pepper, and your favorite barbecue rub or seasoning blend, patting the seasonings onto both sides of the ribs.
3. Wrap and Bake the Ribs:
    - Wrap each rack of ribs tightly in aluminum foil, creating a sealed packet.
    - Place the foil-wrapped ribs on a baking sheet and transfer them to the preheated oven.

- Bake the ribs for 2 1/2 to 3 hours, or until they are tender and cooked through. They should easily pull apart with a fork.

4. Make the Barbecue Sauce:
   - While the ribs are baking, prepare the barbecue sauce. In a medium saucepan, combine the ketchup, apple cider vinegar, brown sugar, Worcestershire sauce, Dijon mustard, smoked paprika, garlic powder, onion powder, and cayenne pepper (if using).
   - Bring the sauce to a simmer over medium heat, then reduce the heat to low and let it cook for 10-15 minutes, stirring occasionally, until the flavors meld together and the sauce thickens slightly.
   - Season the barbecue sauce with salt and black pepper to taste. If you prefer a smoother sauce, you can blend it with an immersion blender or transfer it to a regular blender and puree until smooth.

5. Finish the Ribs:
   - Once the ribs are tender, carefully unwrap them from the foil and discard the foil.
   - Increase the oven temperature to 400°F (200°C).
   - Brush the ribs generously with the prepared barbecue sauce, coating them on both sides.
   - Place the sauced ribs back on the baking sheet and return them to the oven.
   - Bake the ribs for an additional 10-15 minutes, or until the barbecue sauce is caramelized and sticky.

6. Serve:
   - Transfer the barbecue ribs to a cutting board and let them rest for a few minutes before slicing.
   - Serve the ribs hot, optionally with extra barbecue sauce on the side.
   - Enjoy your delicious barbecue ribs with your favorite sides, such as coleslaw, baked beans, or cornbread.

These barbecue ribs are sure to be a hit at any barbecue or gathering, with their tender, flavorful meat and sticky, tangy sauce! Adjust the seasoning and heat level of the barbecue sauce according to your taste preferences.

Chicken and dumplings

Ingredients:

For the chicken:

- 1 whole chicken (about 3-4 pounds), cut into pieces
- Salt and black pepper to taste
- 2 tablespoons vegetable oil
- 1 onion, chopped
- 2 carrots, chopped
- 2 celery stalks, chopped
- 4 cloves garlic, minced
- 8 cups chicken broth (homemade or store-bought)

For the dumplings:

- 2 cups all-purpose flour
- 1 tablespoon baking powder
- 1 teaspoon salt
- 1/4 cup unsalted butter, cold and cubed
- 3/4 cup milk
- Chopped fresh parsley, for garnish (optional)

Instructions:

1. Cook the Chicken:
    - Season the chicken pieces with salt and black pepper.
    - In a large Dutch oven or stockpot, heat the vegetable oil over medium-high heat.
    - Brown the chicken pieces on all sides, working in batches if necessary. Remove the chicken from the pot and set it aside.
2. Sauté the Vegetables:
    - In the same pot, add the chopped onion, carrots, celery, and minced garlic. Sauté until the vegetables are softened, about 5 minutes.
3. Simmer the Broth:
    - Return the browned chicken pieces to the pot.

- Pour in the chicken broth, scraping up any browned bits from the bottom of the pot.
- Bring the broth to a simmer, then reduce the heat to low. Cover and let the chicken simmer gently for about 45 minutes to 1 hour, or until the chicken is cooked through and tender.

4. Make the Dumplings:
   - In a mixing bowl, whisk together the all-purpose flour, baking powder, and salt.
   - Cut in the cold, cubed butter using a pastry cutter or your fingertips, until the mixture resembles coarse crumbs.
   - Gradually add the milk, stirring until a soft dough forms.

5. Add the Dumplings:
   - Once the chicken is cooked, remove it from the pot and shred the meat into bite-sized pieces. Discard the bones and skin.
   - Return the shredded chicken to the pot and bring the broth back to a simmer.
   - Drop spoonfuls of the dumpling dough into the simmering broth, spacing them evenly.
   - Cover the pot and let the dumplings cook for about 15-20 minutes, or until they are cooked through and fluffy.

6. Serve:
   - Ladle the chicken and dumplings into bowls, making sure to include plenty of broth and dumplings.
   - Garnish with chopped fresh parsley if desired.
   - Serve hot and enjoy this comforting Southern classic!

Chicken and dumplings is a hearty and satisfying dish that's perfect for chilly days or whenever you're craving a comforting meal. Adjust the seasoning and thickness of the broth according to your taste preferences.

Grits with cheese

Ingredients:

- 1 cup stone-ground grits
- 4 cups water
- 1 teaspoon salt
- 1 cup shredded cheddar cheese (or your favorite cheese)
- 2 tablespoons unsalted butter
- Salt and black pepper to taste
- Optional toppings: chopped green onions, crumbled bacon, hot sauce

Instructions:

1. Cook the Grits:
    - In a medium saucepan, bring the water to a boil over high heat.
    - Stir in the salt, then gradually whisk in the stone-ground grits, stirring constantly to prevent lumps from forming.
    - Reduce the heat to low and simmer the grits, stirring occasionally, until they are thick and creamy, about 20-25 minutes. Be sure to stir the grits frequently to prevent them from sticking to the bottom of the pan.
2. Add Cheese and Butter:
    - Once the grits are cooked to your desired consistency, remove the saucepan from the heat.
    - Stir in the shredded cheddar cheese and unsalted butter until melted and well combined. The heat from the grits will melt the cheese and butter.
3. Season to Taste:
    - Taste the grits and adjust the seasoning with salt and black pepper as needed.
4. Serve:
    - Serve the cheesy grits hot as a side dish for breakfast, brunch, or dinner.
    - Optionally, garnish with chopped green onions, crumbled bacon, or a drizzle of hot sauce for extra flavor and texture.

Enjoy these creamy and cheesy grits as a comforting and indulgent side dish that pairs well with a variety of dishes, from fried chicken to shrimp and grits. Feel free to customize the recipe by using your favorite cheese or adding other mix-ins to suit your taste preferences.

Cornbread dressing

Ingredients:

For the cornbread:

- 1 cup yellow cornmeal
- 1 cup all-purpose flour
- 1 tablespoon baking powder
- 1 teaspoon salt
- 1 cup buttermilk
- 2 large eggs
- 1/4 cup unsalted butter, melted

For the dressing:

- 8 tablespoons (1 stick) unsalted butter
- 1 large onion, chopped
- 2 celery stalks, chopped
- 2 cloves garlic, minced
- 8 cups crumbled cornbread (about 1 batch of homemade cornbread or store-bought equivalent)
- 2 cups chicken or vegetable broth
- 2 large eggs, beaten
- 2 teaspoons dried sage
- 1 teaspoon dried thyme
- 1 teaspoon dried rosemary
- Salt and black pepper to taste

Instructions:

1. Prepare the Cornbread:
    - Preheat your oven to 400°F (200°C). Grease a 9x9-inch baking dish or cast iron skillet.
    - In a large mixing bowl, whisk together the cornmeal, flour, baking powder, and salt.
    - In another bowl, whisk together the buttermilk, eggs, and melted butter.

- Pour the wet ingredients into the dry ingredients and stir until just combined. Be careful not to overmix.
- Pour the batter into the prepared baking dish or skillet and spread it out evenly.
- Bake for 20-25 minutes, or until the cornbread is golden brown and a toothpick inserted into the center comes out clean.
- Remove from the oven and let cool completely. Once cooled, crumble the cornbread into a large mixing bowl.

2. Prepare the Dressing:
    - Lower the oven temperature to 350°F (175°C).
    - In a large skillet, melt the butter over medium heat. Add the chopped onion and celery, and cook until softened, about 5-7 minutes. Add the minced garlic and cook for an additional 1-2 minutes.
    - Add the cooked onion, celery, and garlic mixture to the crumbled cornbread in the mixing bowl.
    - Stir in the chicken or vegetable broth until the cornbread is moistened but not soggy.
    - Add the beaten eggs, dried sage, dried thyme, dried rosemary, salt, and black pepper to the bowl. Stir until everything is well combined.
3. Bake the Dressing:
    - Transfer the dressing mixture to a greased 9x13-inch baking dish.
    - Cover the baking dish with aluminum foil and bake for 30 minutes.
    - Remove the foil and bake for an additional 20-25 minutes, or until the dressing is golden brown and crispy on top.
4. Serve:
    - Let the cornbread dressing cool for a few minutes before serving.
    - Serve warm as a delicious side dish alongside your favorite holiday meal.

Enjoy this classic Southern cornbread dressing as a comforting and flavorful addition to your holiday table! Feel free to customize the recipe by adding other ingredients such as cooked sausage, dried cranberries, or chopped pecans to suit your taste preferences.

Beignets

Ingredients:

- 1 cup lukewarm water
- 1/4 cup granulated sugar
- 1 packet (2 1/4 teaspoons) active dry yeast
- 1 large egg, beaten
- 1/2 cup evaporated milk
- 4 cups all-purpose flour
- 1/2 teaspoon salt
- Vegetable oil, for frying
- Powdered sugar, for dusting

Instructions:

1. Activate the Yeast:
    - In a large mixing bowl, combine the lukewarm water, granulated sugar, and active dry yeast. Let the mixture sit for about 5-10 minutes, or until the yeast becomes foamy and activated.
2. Prepare the Dough:
    - Once the yeast is activated, stir in the beaten egg and evaporated milk.
    - Gradually add the all-purpose flour and salt to the bowl, stirring until a sticky dough forms.
3. Knead the Dough:
    - Turn the dough out onto a lightly floured surface and knead it for about 5 minutes, or until it becomes smooth and elastic. Add more flour if necessary to prevent sticking.
4. Let the Dough Rise:
    - Place the kneaded dough in a greased bowl and cover it with a clean kitchen towel or plastic wrap.
    - Let the dough rise in a warm, draft-free place for about 1-2 hours, or until it doubles in size.
5. Roll and Cut the Beignets:
    - After the dough has risen, punch it down and roll it out on a floured surface to about 1/4 inch thickness.
    - Use a sharp knife or pizza cutter to cut the dough into squares or rectangles, about 2-3 inches in size.
6. Fry the Beignets:

- In a deep fryer or heavy-bottomed pot, heat vegetable oil to 350°F (175°C).
- Carefully place the cut beignet dough into the hot oil, a few pieces at a time, being careful not to overcrowd the pot.
- Fry the beignets for about 2-3 minutes per side, or until they are puffed up and golden brown.
- Use a slotted spoon or spider strainer to remove the fried beignets from the oil and drain them on paper towels.

7. Serve:
    - Dust the warm beignets generously with powdered sugar.
    - Serve the beignets hot and enjoy them as a delicious breakfast or dessert treat.

Beignets are best enjoyed fresh and hot, so serve them immediately after frying for the best flavor and texture. These light and airy pastries are sure to be a hit with family and friends!

Bourbon-glazed ham

Ingredients:

- 1 (8-10 pound) bone-in fully cooked ham
- 1 cup bourbon
- 1 cup brown sugar
- 1/2 cup honey
- 1/4 cup Dijon mustard
- 1/4 cup apple cider vinegar
- 1 tablespoon Worcestershire sauce
- 1 teaspoon ground cloves
- 1/2 teaspoon ground cinnamon
- 1/4 teaspoon ground nutmeg
- Salt and black pepper to taste

Instructions:

1. Prepare the Ham:
    - Preheat your oven to 325°F (160°C).
    - Place the ham in a large roasting pan, cut side down.
    - Score the surface of the ham in a diamond pattern with a sharp knife, making shallow cuts about 1/4 inch deep.
2. Make the Bourbon Glaze:
    - In a saucepan, combine the bourbon, brown sugar, honey, Dijon mustard, apple cider vinegar, Worcestershire sauce, ground cloves, ground cinnamon, and ground nutmeg.
    - Bring the mixture to a simmer over medium heat, stirring occasionally.
    - Let the glaze simmer for about 10-15 minutes, or until it thickens slightly and reduces to a syrupy consistency. Remove from heat.
3. Glaze the Ham:
    - Brush a generous amount of the bourbon glaze all over the surface of the scored ham, making sure to get the glaze into the cuts.
    - Season the ham lightly with salt and black pepper.
4. Bake the Ham:
    - Place the ham in the preheated oven and bake uncovered for about 1 1/2 to 2 hours, or until heated through and the internal temperature reaches

140°F (60°C) on a meat thermometer, basting with the bourbon glaze every 30 minutes.
5. Serve:
    - Once the ham is cooked through and glazed to perfection, remove it from the oven and let it rest for about 10-15 minutes before slicing.
    - Slice the ham and serve it warm, drizzling any remaining bourbon glaze over the slices.

Enjoy the deliciously tender and flavorful bourbon-glazed ham as the centerpiece of your holiday table or special occasion meal. The sweet and savory glaze pairs perfectly with the smoky, salty flavor of the ham, making it a standout dish that's sure to impress!

Shrimp and sausage jambalaya

Ingredients:

- 1 pound large shrimp, peeled and deveined
- 1/2 pound smoked sausage (such as Andouille), sliced
- 1 onion, chopped
- 1 bell pepper, chopped
- 2 celery stalks, chopped
- 3 cloves garlic, minced
- 1 cup long-grain white rice
- 1 (14.5 oz) can diced tomatoes
- 2 cups chicken broth
- 2 teaspoons Cajun seasoning (store-bought or homemade)
- 1 teaspoon dried thyme
- 1 teaspoon paprika
- 1/2 teaspoon dried oregano
- 1/4 teaspoon cayenne pepper (optional, for heat)
- Salt and black pepper to taste
- Chopped green onions, for garnish
- Chopped fresh parsley, for garnish

Instructions:

1. Sauté the Sausage and Vegetables:
    - Heat a large skillet or Dutch oven over medium heat. Add the sliced sausage and cook until browned, about 5 minutes.
    - Add the chopped onion, bell pepper, and celery to the skillet. Sauté until the vegetables are softened, about 5-7 minutes.
    - Stir in the minced garlic and cook for an additional 1-2 minutes until fragrant.
2. Add Rice and Seasonings:
    - Add the long-grain white rice to the skillet, stirring to coat it with the sausage and vegetable mixture.
    - Stir in the diced tomatoes (with their juices), chicken broth, Cajun seasoning, dried thyme, paprika, dried oregano, and cayenne pepper (if using).

- Season the mixture with salt and black pepper to taste. Bring the mixture to a boil.
3. Simmer:
    - Once the mixture comes to a boil, reduce the heat to low and cover the skillet. Let the jambalaya simmer for about 15-20 minutes, or until the rice is tender and most of the liquid has been absorbed.
4. Add Shrimp:
    - Once the rice is almost cooked through, add the peeled and deveined shrimp to the skillet. Stir the shrimp into the rice mixture.
    - Cover the skillet and continue to cook for an additional 5-7 minutes, or until the shrimp are pink and cooked through.
5. Serve:
    - Once the shrimp are cooked through and the rice is tender, remove the skillet from the heat.
    - Garnish the shrimp and sausage jambalaya with chopped green onions and fresh parsley before serving.
    - Serve hot and enjoy this flavorful and comforting dish!

Shrimp and sausage jambalaya is a delicious one-pot meal that's perfect for weeknight dinners or entertaining guests. Adjust the seasoning and spice level according to your taste preferences, and feel free to add additional vegetables or protein to customize the dish to your liking.

Key lime pie

Ingredients:

For the crust:

- 1 1/2 cups graham cracker crumbs
- 1/4 cup granulated sugar
- 1/2 cup unsalted butter, melted

For the filling:

- 4 large egg yolks
- 1 (14-ounce) can sweetened condensed milk
- 1/2 cup fresh key lime juice (about 15-20 key limes)
- 1 tablespoon key lime zest (optional, for extra flavor)

For the topping (optional):

- 1 cup heavy cream
- 2 tablespoons powdered sugar
- Additional key lime zest for garnish

Instructions:

1. Preheat the Oven:
    - Preheat your oven to 350°F (175°C).
2. Make the Crust:
    - In a mixing bowl, combine the graham cracker crumbs, granulated sugar, and melted butter. Stir until the mixture resembles wet sand and holds together when pressed.
    - Press the crumb mixture evenly into the bottom and up the sides of a 9-inch pie dish.
    - Bake the crust in the preheated oven for 8-10 minutes, or until lightly golden and set. Remove from the oven and let it cool slightly.
3. Make the Filling:

- In a separate mixing bowl, whisk together the egg yolks and sweetened condensed milk until smooth.
- Gradually whisk in the key lime juice and key lime zest (if using) until well combined and the mixture is smooth.

4. Assemble and Bake the Pie:
   - Pour the key lime filling into the pre-baked graham cracker crust, spreading it out evenly.
   - Return the pie to the oven and bake for an additional 10-12 minutes, or until the filling is set and slightly firm to the touch.
   - Remove the pie from the oven and let it cool to room temperature. Then, refrigerate it for at least 2 hours, or until chilled and set.

5. Make the Topping (Optional):
   - In a mixing bowl, whip the heavy cream and powdered sugar together until stiff peaks form.
   - Spread or pipe the whipped cream over the chilled key lime pie.
   - Garnish the pie with additional key lime zest, if desired.

6. Serve:
   - Slice the key lime pie into wedges and serve chilled.
   - Enjoy this tangy and refreshing dessert as a perfect ending to any meal!

Key lime pie is best enjoyed chilled and can be stored in the refrigerator for up to 3-4 days. It's a wonderful treat for any occasion, with its creamy filling and buttery graham cracker crust.

Shrimp and grits casserole

Ingredients:

For the grits:

- 1 cup stone-ground grits
- 4 cups water or chicken broth
- Salt and black pepper to taste
- 1/2 cup shredded cheddar cheese
- 2 tablespoons unsalted butter

For the shrimp:

- 1 pound shrimp, peeled and deveined
- 2 cloves garlic, minced
- 1 tablespoon Cajun seasoning (or to taste)
- 2 tablespoons unsalted butter
- 2 tablespoons all-purpose flour
- 1 cup chicken broth
- 1/2 cup heavy cream
- 1/2 cup shredded cheddar cheese
- Salt and black pepper to taste

For the topping:

- 4 slices bacon, cooked and crumbled
- Chopped green onions for garnish

Instructions:

1. Prepare the Grits:
    - In a medium saucepan, bring the water or chicken broth to a boil over medium-high heat.
    - Gradually whisk in the stone-ground grits, stirring constantly to prevent lumps from forming.

- Reduce the heat to low and simmer the grits, stirring occasionally, until they are thick and creamy, about 20-25 minutes.
- Stir in the shredded cheddar cheese, butter, salt, and black pepper until the cheese is melted and the grits are smooth. Remove from heat.

2. Prepare the Shrimp:
    - Preheat your oven to 375°F (190°C).
    - In a large skillet, melt the butter over medium heat. Add the minced garlic and cook for 1-2 minutes, until fragrant.
    - Add the shrimp to the skillet and sprinkle with Cajun seasoning. Cook the shrimp for 2-3 minutes on each side, until pink and cooked through. Remove the shrimp from the skillet and set aside.
    - In the same skillet, add the flour and cook, stirring constantly, for 1-2 minutes to make a roux.
    - Gradually whisk in the chicken broth and heavy cream until smooth. Bring the mixture to a simmer and cook for 2-3 minutes, until thickened.
    - Stir in the shredded cheddar cheese until melted and smooth. Season with salt and black pepper to taste.

3. Assemble the Casserole:
    - In a greased 9x13-inch baking dish, spread half of the cooked grits into an even layer.
    - Arrange the cooked shrimp on top of the grits in an even layer.
    - Pour the cheese sauce over the shrimp and spread it out evenly.
    - Top the casserole with the remaining cooked grits, spreading them into an even layer.

4. Bake the Casserole:
    - Place the baking dish in the preheated oven and bake for 20-25 minutes, until the casserole is heated through and bubbly.
    - Remove the casserole from the oven and sprinkle the crumbled bacon over the top.

5. Serve:
    - Garnish the shrimp and grits casserole with chopped green onions before serving.
    - Serve hot and enjoy this delicious and comforting Southern dish!

This shrimp and grits casserole is perfect for brunch, lunch, or dinner and is sure to satisfy your craving for classic Southern flavors. Feel free to customize the recipe by adding your favorite seasonings or toppings.

Fried okra

Ingredients:

- 1 pound fresh okra
- 1 cup cornmeal or all-purpose flour
- 1 teaspoon salt
- 1/2 teaspoon black pepper
- 1/2 teaspoon garlic powder
- 1/2 teaspoon paprika (optional, for extra flavor)
- Vegetable oil, for frying

Instructions:

1. Prepare the Okra:
    - Rinse the okra under cold water and pat it dry with paper towels.
    - Trim off the stem ends of the okra pods, then slice them into 1/2-inch rounds.
2. Coat the Okra:
    - In a shallow dish or bowl, combine the cornmeal or flour with salt, black pepper, garlic powder, and paprika (if using). Stir until well combined.
    - Add the sliced okra to the cornmeal or flour mixture, tossing to coat each piece evenly.
3. Fry the Okra:
    - In a large skillet or deep fryer, heat vegetable oil to 350°F (175°C) over medium heat.
    - Once the oil is hot, carefully add the coated okra to the skillet in batches, making sure not to overcrowd the pan.
    - Fry the okra for 3-4 minutes, stirring occasionally, until golden brown and crispy.
    - Use a slotted spoon or spider strainer to transfer the fried okra to a paper towel-lined plate to drain excess oil.
    - Repeat the frying process with the remaining batches of okra until all the slices are cooked.
4. Serve:
    - Serve the fried okra hot as a side dish or appetizer.
    - Enjoy it on its own or with your favorite dipping sauce, such as ranch dressing or remoulade.

Fried okra is best served immediately while it's still hot and crispy. It makes a delicious addition to any Southern meal and is sure to be a hit with family and friends!

Boudin sausage

Ingredients:

- 1 pound pork shoulder, cut into small pieces
- 1/4 pound pork liver, diced
- 1 cup uncooked white rice
- 1 large onion, finely chopped
- 2 cloves garlic, minced
- 1 green bell pepper, finely chopped
- 2 stalks celery, finely chopped
- 2 green onions, thinly sliced
- 2 tablespoons fresh parsley, chopped
- 1 teaspoon salt
- 1/2 teaspoon black pepper
- 1/2 teaspoon cayenne pepper (adjust to taste)
- 1/2 teaspoon paprika
- 1/2 teaspoon dried thyme
- 1/2 teaspoon dried oregano
- Hog casings (optional, for stuffing)
- Vegetable oil, for cooking

Instructions:

1. Cook the Rice:
    - In a medium saucepan, cook the white rice according to package instructions. Once cooked, set aside to cool.
2. Prepare the Meat Mixture:
    - In a large skillet or Dutch oven, heat a tablespoon of vegetable oil over medium heat.
    - Add the diced pork shoulder and pork liver to the skillet, and cook until browned and cooked through, about 8-10 minutes.
    - Add the chopped onion, garlic, green bell pepper, and celery to the skillet, and cook until the vegetables are softened, about 5 minutes.
    - Stir in the cooked rice, green onions, parsley, salt, black pepper, cayenne pepper, paprika, dried thyme, and dried oregano. Mix until well combined.
    - Remove the skillet from the heat and let the mixture cool slightly.
3. Stuff the Casings (Optional):

- If using hog casings, rinse them thoroughly under cold water and soak them in warm water for about 30 minutes to soften.
- Use a sausage stuffer to fill the hog casings with the boudin mixture, tying off the ends to form individual sausages. Alternatively, you can simply shape the mixture into patties if you prefer.

4. Cook the Boudin:
    - To cook the boudin, you can either boil it or grill it.
    - To boil: Bring a large pot of water to a boil. Add the boudin sausages or patties to the boiling water and cook for about 15-20 minutes, or until heated through.
    - To grill: Preheat your grill to medium-high heat. Grill the boudin sausages or patties for about 5-7 minutes per side, or until they are browned and heated through.
5. Serve:
    - Once cooked, serve the boudin hot as a main dish or appetizer.
    - Enjoy it on its own or with your favorite Cajun condiments, such as hot sauce or mustard.

Boudin sausage is a delicious and flavorful dish that showcases the unique flavors of Cajun cuisine. It's perfect for a casual meal or as part of a festive gathering with friends and family. Adjust the seasoning and spice level according to your taste preferences.

Cajun dirty rice

Ingredients:

- 1 cup long-grain white rice
- 2 cups chicken or beef broth
- 1 pound ground pork, chicken, or beef
- 1 onion, finely chopped
- 1 bell pepper, finely chopped
- 2 celery stalks, finely chopped
- 3 cloves garlic, minced
- 2 green onions, thinly sliced
- 1/4 cup fresh parsley, chopped
- 2 tablespoons vegetable oil
- 2 teaspoons Cajun seasoning
- 1 teaspoon paprika
- 1/2 teaspoon dried thyme
- Salt and black pepper to taste

Instructions:

1. Cook the Rice:
    - Rinse the white rice under cold water until the water runs clear.
    - In a medium saucepan, bring the chicken or beef broth to a boil over medium-high heat.
    - Stir in the rinsed rice, reduce the heat to low, cover, and simmer for about 18-20 minutes, or until the rice is cooked and the liquid is absorbed.
    - Remove the saucepan from the heat and let the rice rest, covered, for 5 minutes. Fluff the rice with a fork and set it aside.
2. Prepare the Meat Mixture:
    - In a large skillet or Dutch oven, heat the vegetable oil over medium heat.
    - Add the ground meat to the skillet and cook, breaking it up with a spoon, until browned and cooked through, about 5-7 minutes.
    - Add the chopped onion, bell pepper, and celery to the skillet with the cooked meat. Cook, stirring occasionally, until the vegetables are softened, about 5 minutes.
    - Stir in the minced garlic and cook for an additional 1-2 minutes until fragrant.
3. Season and Combine:

- Add the cooked rice to the skillet with the meat and vegetables.
- Stir in the Cajun seasoning, paprika, dried thyme, green onions, and chopped parsley.
- Season the mixture with salt and black pepper to taste. Stir well to combine all the ingredients.

4. Cook and Serve:
    - Cook the dirty rice mixture for an additional 5-7 minutes, stirring occasionally, until heated through and the flavors have melded together.
    - Taste and adjust the seasoning, if needed.
    - Once heated through, remove the skillet from the heat.
    - Serve the Cajun dirty rice hot as a delicious and satisfying main dish or side.

Cajun dirty rice is a flavorful and comforting dish that's perfect for any occasion. It's a great way to enjoy the bold and spicy flavors of Cajun cuisine, and it pairs well with a variety of meats and seafood. Feel free to customize the recipe by adding your favorite ingredients or adjusting the level of spiciness to suit your taste preferences.

Sweet potato pie

Ingredients:

For the crust:

- 1 1/4 cups all-purpose flour
- 1/2 teaspoon salt
- 1/2 teaspoon granulated sugar
- 1/2 cup cold unsalted butter, cut into small cubes
- 3-4 tablespoons ice water

For the filling:

- 2 cups mashed sweet potatoes (about 2 medium sweet potatoes)
- 3/4 cup granulated sugar
- 1/2 cup packed brown sugar
- 2 large eggs, beaten
- 1/2 cup evaporated milk
- 1/4 cup unsalted butter, melted
- 1 teaspoon vanilla extract
- 1/2 teaspoon ground cinnamon
- 1/4 teaspoon ground nutmeg
- 1/4 teaspoon ground cloves
- 1/4 teaspoon salt

Instructions:

1. Prepare the Crust:
   - In a large mixing bowl, whisk together the flour, salt, and granulated sugar.
   - Add the cold cubed butter to the flour mixture. Using a pastry cutter or your fingers, work the butter into the flour until the mixture resembles coarse crumbs.
   - Gradually add the ice water, 1 tablespoon at a time, mixing until the dough comes together and forms a ball. Be careful not to overwork the dough.
   - Shape the dough into a disk, wrap it in plastic wrap, and refrigerate for at least 30 minutes.
2. Preheat the Oven:
   - Preheat your oven to 375°F (190°C).

3. Roll out the Crust:
   - On a lightly floured surface, roll out the chilled dough into a circle about 12 inches in diameter.
   - Carefully transfer the rolled-out dough to a 9-inch pie dish. Trim any excess dough from the edges and crimp the edges decoratively. Refrigerate the crust while you prepare the filling.
4. Prepare the Filling:
   - In a large mixing bowl, combine the mashed sweet potatoes, granulated sugar, brown sugar, beaten eggs, evaporated milk, melted butter, vanilla extract, ground cinnamon, ground nutmeg, ground cloves, and salt. Mix until smooth and well combined.
5. Assemble and Bake the Pie:
   - Pour the sweet potato filling into the prepared pie crust, spreading it out evenly.
   - Place the pie in the preheated oven and bake for 50-60 minutes, or until the filling is set and the crust is golden brown.
   - If the edges of the crust start to brown too quickly, you can cover them with aluminum foil halfway through baking to prevent burning.
6. Cool and Serve:
   - Once baked, remove the pie from the oven and let it cool completely on a wire rack before slicing and serving.
   - Serve the sweet potato pie at room temperature or chilled, topped with whipped cream or vanilla ice cream, if desired.

Enjoy this deliciously comforting sweet potato pie as a perfect ending to any meal, especially during the holiday season!

Texas chili

Ingredients:

- 2 pounds beef chuck roast, cut into 1/2-inch cubes
- 2 tablespoons vegetable oil
- 2 onions, chopped
- 4 cloves garlic, minced
- 2-3 jalapeño peppers, seeded and finely chopped (adjust to taste)
- 2 tablespoons chili powder
- 1 tablespoon ground cumin
- 1 teaspoon dried oregano
- 1 teaspoon paprika
- 1/2 teaspoon cayenne pepper (adjust to taste)
- 1/2 teaspoon ground black pepper
- 1/2 teaspoon salt
- 1 (28-ounce) can crushed tomatoes
- 1 cup beef broth or water
- Optional toppings: shredded cheese, chopped onions, sour cream, cilantro, lime wedges

Instructions:

1. Brown the Beef:
    - Heat the vegetable oil in a large Dutch oven or heavy-bottomed pot over medium-high heat.
    - Add the cubed beef to the pot in batches, making sure not to overcrowd the pan, and cook until browned on all sides. Remove the browned beef from the pot and set aside.
2. Cook the Aromatics:
    - In the same pot, add the chopped onions and cook until softened, about 5 minutes.
    - Add the minced garlic and chopped jalapeño peppers to the pot and cook for an additional 2 minutes, until fragrant.
3. Add the Spices:
    - Stir in the chili powder, ground cumin, dried oregano, paprika, cayenne pepper, ground black pepper, and salt. Cook the spices for 1-2 minutes to toast them and enhance their flavor.
4. Simmer the Chili:

- Return the browned beef to the pot and stir to combine with the onion and spice mixture.
- Pour in the crushed tomatoes and beef broth or water, stirring to combine.
- Bring the chili to a boil, then reduce the heat to low and let it simmer, partially covered, for 1 1/2 to 2 hours, stirring occasionally, until the beef is tender and the flavors have melded together. Add more broth or water if needed to reach your desired consistency.

5. Serve:
   - Once the chili is cooked to your liking, taste and adjust the seasoning as needed.
   - Ladle the Texas chili into bowls and serve hot.
   - Garnish with your favorite toppings, such as shredded cheese, chopped onions, sour cream, cilantro, or lime wedges.

Enjoy this rich and flavorful Texas chili on its own or with a side of cornbread for a satisfying meal, perfect for cozy evenings or game day gatherings!

Southern-style coleslaw

Ingredients:

- 1 small head of cabbage, finely shredded (about 4 cups)
- 1 large carrot, grated
- 1/2 cup mayonnaise
- 2 tablespoons apple cider vinegar
- 1 tablespoon granulated sugar
- 1 teaspoon Dijon mustard
- 1/2 teaspoon celery seed (optional)
- Salt and black pepper to taste

Instructions:

1. Prepare the Vegetables:
    - Wash the cabbage and remove any tough outer leaves. Cut the cabbage in half and remove the core. Finely shred the cabbage using a sharp knife or a mandoline slicer.
    - Peel the carrot and grate it using a box grater or a food processor fitted with a grating attachment.
2. Make the Dressing:
    - In a small bowl, whisk together the mayonnaise, apple cider vinegar, granulated sugar, Dijon mustard, and celery seed (if using) until smooth and well combined.
    - Season the dressing with salt and black pepper to taste. Adjust the seasoning to suit your preferences.
3. Combine the Ingredients:
    - In a large mixing bowl, combine the shredded cabbage and grated carrot.
    - Pour the prepared dressing over the cabbage and carrot mixture.
    - Toss the ingredients together until the cabbage and carrot are evenly coated with the dressing.
4. Chill and Serve:
    - Cover the bowl with plastic wrap and refrigerate the coleslaw for at least 1 hour, or until chilled, to allow the flavors to meld together.
    - Before serving, give the coleslaw a final toss to ensure that the dressing is evenly distributed.

- Serve the Southern-style coleslaw as a side dish alongside grilled meats, sandwiches, or fried chicken.

Enjoy this deliciously creamy and refreshing coleslaw with its classic Southern flavors. It's the perfect accompaniment to a wide variety of dishes and adds a cool and crunchy element to any meal!

Gooey butter cake

Ingredients:

For the cake base:

- 1 box (about 15.25 ounces) yellow cake mix
- 1/2 cup (1 stick) unsalted butter, melted
- 1 large egg

For the gooey filling:

- 1 package (8 ounces) cream cheese, softened
- 2 large eggs
- 1 teaspoon vanilla extract
- 1/2 cup (1 stick) unsalted butter, melted
- 1 box (16 ounces) powdered sugar, sifted

Instructions:

1. Preheat the Oven:
    - Preheat your oven to 350°F (175°C). Grease a 9x13-inch baking dish and set it aside.
2. Prepare the Cake Base:
    - In a large mixing bowl, combine the yellow cake mix, melted butter, and egg. Stir until well combined and a thick dough forms.
    - Press the cake mixture evenly into the bottom of the prepared baking dish, forming a smooth and compact layer.
3. Make the Gooey Filling:
    - In another mixing bowl, beat the softened cream cheese until smooth and creamy.
    - Add the eggs and vanilla extract to the cream cheese, and beat until well combined.
    - Gradually add the melted butter to the cream cheese mixture, beating until smooth.
    - Slowly add the sifted powdered sugar to the cream cheese mixture, beating until smooth and well incorporated.

4. Assemble and Bake:
   - Pour the gooey filling over the cake base in the baking dish, spreading it out evenly with a spatula.
   - Bake the gooey butter cake in the preheated oven for 40-45 minutes, or until the edges are golden brown and the center is set but still slightly gooey.
   - Remove the cake from the oven and let it cool completely in the baking dish on a wire rack.
5. Serve:
   - Once cooled, cut the gooey butter cake into squares or rectangles.
   - Dust the top with powdered sugar, if desired, before serving.
   - Serve the gooey butter cake at room temperature and enjoy its rich and indulgent flavor!

This gooey butter cake is a crowd-pleasing dessert that's perfect for special occasions or any time you're craving something sweet and satisfying. Its irresistible combination of buttery cake and creamy filling is sure to be a hit with family and friends!

Cajun fried turkey

Ingredients:

- 1 whole turkey (12-14 pounds), thawed if frozen
- Cajun seasoning (store-bought or homemade)
- 2 gallons peanut oil (or other high smoke point oil), for frying
- Injection marinade (optional, for added flavor and moisture)

For the Injection Marinade (optional):

- 1 cup chicken broth
- 1/2 cup unsalted butter, melted
- 2 tablespoons Cajun seasoning

Instructions:

1. Prepare the Turkey:
   - If using, prepare the injection marinade by combining the chicken broth, melted butter, and Cajun seasoning in a bowl. Use a meat injector to inject the marinade into various parts of the turkey, such as the breast, thighs, and legs, to add flavor and moisture. Refrigerate the turkey for at least 2 hours, or overnight, to allow the flavors to meld.
2. Season the Turkey:
   - Remove the turkey from the refrigerator and pat it dry with paper towels.
   - Liberally season the turkey, inside and out, with Cajun seasoning, making sure to coat all surfaces evenly. You can use a store-bought Cajun seasoning blend or make your own by combining salt, black pepper, garlic powder, onion powder, paprika, cayenne pepper, and other spices according to your taste preferences.
3. Preheat the Oil:
   - In a large turkey fryer pot or deep fryer, heat the peanut oil to 350°F (175°C) over medium-high heat. Use a candy or deep-fry thermometer to monitor the temperature of the oil.
4. Fry the Turkey:
   - Once the oil reaches the proper temperature, carefully lower the seasoned turkey into the hot oil using a turkey fryer basket or sturdy kitchen utensils. Be sure to wear protective gloves and stand back to avoid splatters.

- Fry the turkey for about 3-4 minutes per pound, or until it reaches an internal temperature of 165°F (74°C) in the thickest part of the breast and thighs. Make sure to monitor the temperature of the oil and adjust the heat as needed to maintain a consistent frying temperature.
- Once the turkey is cooked through and golden brown, carefully remove it from the hot oil and transfer it to a cutting board or serving platter.

5. Rest and Serve:
    - Allow the fried turkey to rest for 15-20 minutes before carving to allow the juices to redistribute.
    - Carve the turkey into slices or pieces, and serve it hot with your favorite side dishes, such as mashed potatoes, gravy, stuffing, and cranberry sauce.

Cajun fried turkey is a delicious and impressive dish that's sure to be a hit at any gathering. Enjoy the spicy Cajun flavors and crispy skin for a memorable dining experience! Remember to follow safety precautions when deep-frying a turkey, including using a properly sized fryer and frying outdoors in a well-ventilated area away from flammable materials.

Chicken bog

Ingredients:

- 1 whole chicken (about 3-4 pounds), cut into pieces
- 1 pound smoked sausage (such as kielbasa or Andouille), sliced
- 1 onion, chopped
- 2 cloves garlic, minced
- 2 cups long-grain white rice
- 6 cups chicken broth or water
- 1 teaspoon salt, or to taste
- 1/2 teaspoon black pepper, or to taste
- 1/2 teaspoon paprika
- 1/4 teaspoon cayenne pepper (optional, for heat)
- Chopped fresh parsley, for garnish

Instructions:

1. Brown the Chicken and Sausage:
    - In a large Dutch oven or heavy-bottomed pot, heat a tablespoon of oil over medium-high heat.
    - Add the chicken pieces to the pot and brown them on all sides, about 5-7 minutes per side. Remove the browned chicken from the pot and set it aside.
    - In the same pot, add the sliced smoked sausage and cook until browned, about 5 minutes. Remove the sausage from the pot and set it aside.
2. Saute the Aromatics:
    - In the same pot, add the chopped onion and cook until softened, about 5 minutes.
    - Add the minced garlic to the pot and cook for an additional 1-2 minutes, until fragrant.
3. Combine Ingredients:
    - Return the browned chicken and sausage to the pot with the sautéed onions and garlic.
    - Add the long-grain white rice to the pot and stir to combine with the other ingredients.
4. Season and Simmer:

- Pour the chicken broth or water into the pot, ensuring that the rice and meat are fully submerged.
- Season the mixture with salt, black pepper, paprika, and cayenne pepper (if using). Stir well to combine.
- Bring the mixture to a boil over high heat, then reduce the heat to low. Cover the pot with a lid and let it simmer for about 30-40 minutes, or until the rice is cooked and the chicken is tender.

5. Serve:
    - Once cooked, remove the chicken pieces from the pot and shred the meat using two forks. Discard the bones and return the shredded chicken to the pot.
    - Stir the chicken bog mixture well to combine all the ingredients.
    - Taste and adjust the seasoning, if needed.
    - Serve the chicken bog hot, garnished with chopped fresh parsley for a pop of color.

Chicken bog is a comforting and satisfying dish that's perfect for feeding a crowd or enjoying as a cozy family meal. It's simple to prepare and packed with delicious flavors that everyone will love!

Chocolate pecan pie

Ingredients:

For the pie crust:

- 1 1/4 cups all-purpose flour
- 1/2 teaspoon salt
- 1/2 teaspoon granulated sugar
- 1/2 cup (1 stick) cold unsalted butter, cut into small cubes
- 3-4 tablespoons ice water

For the filling:

- 1 cup light corn syrup
- 3/4 cup packed light brown sugar
- 3 large eggs
- 1 teaspoon vanilla extract
- 2 tablespoons unsalted butter, melted
- 1 tablespoon all-purpose flour
- 1/4 teaspoon salt
- 1 cup semi-sweet chocolate chips
- 1 1/2 cups pecan halves

Instructions:

1. Prepare the Pie Crust:
    - In a large mixing bowl, combine the flour, salt, and granulated sugar.
    - Add the cold cubed butter to the flour mixture. Using a pastry cutter or your fingers, work the butter into the flour until the mixture resembles coarse crumbs.
    - Gradually add the ice water, 1 tablespoon at a time, mixing until the dough comes together and forms a ball. Be careful not to overwork the dough.
    - Shape the dough into a disk, wrap it in plastic wrap, and refrigerate for at least 30 minutes.
2. Preheat the Oven:

- Preheat your oven to 350°F (175°C). Place a baking sheet in the oven to preheat as well.

3. Roll out the Crust:
    - On a lightly floured surface, roll out the chilled dough into a circle about 12 inches in diameter.
    - Carefully transfer the rolled-out dough to a 9-inch pie dish. Trim any excess dough from the edges and crimp the edges decoratively. Refrigerate the crust while you prepare the filling.
4. Make the Filling:
    - In a large mixing bowl, whisk together the corn syrup, light brown sugar, eggs, vanilla extract, melted butter, flour, and salt until smooth and well combined.
    - Stir in the semi-sweet chocolate chips and pecan halves until evenly distributed throughout the filling mixture.
5. Assemble and Bake the Pie:
    - Pour the filling into the prepared pie crust, spreading it out evenly with a spatula.
    - Place the pie on the preheated baking sheet in the oven and bake for 50-60 minutes, or until the filling is set and the crust is golden brown. If the crust starts to brown too quickly, you can cover the edges with aluminum foil halfway through baking.
    - Once baked, remove the pie from the oven and let it cool completely on a wire rack before slicing and serving.
6. Serve:
    - Serve the chocolate pecan pie slices at room temperature or slightly warmed, optionally topped with whipped cream or a scoop of vanilla ice cream.

Enjoy this indulgent chocolate pecan pie as a delicious dessert for any occasion, especially during the holiday season!

Brunswick stew

Ingredients:

- 2 tablespoons vegetable oil
- 1 pound boneless chicken thighs, diced
- 1 pound pork shoulder, diced
- Salt and pepper to taste
- 1 onion, chopped
- 2 cloves garlic, minced
- 2 cups chicken broth
- 1 can (14.5 ounces) diced tomatoes, undrained
- 2 cups fresh or frozen corn kernels
- 2 cups lima beans (fresh or frozen)
- 2 cups diced potatoes
- 1 cup diced carrots
- 1/4 cup Worcestershire sauce
- 1/4 cup ketchup
- 2 tablespoons apple cider vinegar
- 1 tablespoon brown sugar
- 1 teaspoon smoked paprika
- 1/2 teaspoon dried thyme
- 1/4 teaspoon cayenne pepper (optional, for heat)
- Chopped fresh parsley or green onions, for garnish

Instructions:

1. Brown the Meat:
    - Heat the vegetable oil in a large pot or Dutch oven over medium-high heat.
    - Season the diced chicken thighs and pork shoulder with salt and pepper.
    - Add the diced chicken and pork to the pot and cook until browned on all sides. Remove the browned meat from the pot and set it aside.
2. Saute the Aromatics:
    - In the same pot, add the chopped onion and minced garlic. Cook until softened and fragrant, about 3-4 minutes.
3. Simmer the Stew:
    - Return the browned meat to the pot with the sauteed onion and garlic.

- Add the chicken broth, diced tomatoes (with their juices), corn kernels, lima beans, diced potatoes, diced carrots, Worcestershire sauce, ketchup, apple cider vinegar, brown sugar, smoked paprika, dried thyme, and cayenne pepper (if using). Stir to combine.
- Bring the mixture to a boil, then reduce the heat to low. Cover the pot and let the stew simmer for about 1 to 1 1/2 hours, stirring occasionally, until the meat is tender and the vegetables are cooked through. Add more broth or water if needed to reach your desired consistency.

4. Adjust Seasoning and Serve:
    - Taste the stew and adjust the seasoning with salt, pepper, or additional seasonings as needed.
    - Serve the Brunswick stew hot, garnished with chopped fresh parsley or green onions.

Enjoy this delicious and comforting Brunswick stew with crusty bread or cornbread for a satisfying meal that's sure to warm you up on a cold day!

Fried pickles

Ingredients:

- 1 jar dill pickle slices, drained and patted dry
- 1 cup all-purpose flour
- 1 teaspoon paprika
- 1/2 teaspoon garlic powder
- 1/2 teaspoon onion powder
- 1/4 teaspoon cayenne pepper (optional, for heat)
- Salt and black pepper to taste
- 1 cup buttermilk
- 1 large egg
- 1 cup breadcrumbs or cornmeal
- Vegetable oil, for frying
- Ranch dressing, spicy mayo, or other dipping sauce of your choice

Instructions:

1. Prepare the Pickles:
    - Drain the pickle slices from the jar and pat them dry with paper towels to remove excess moisture. Set aside.
2. Set Up the Breading Station:
    - In one shallow dish, combine the all-purpose flour, paprika, garlic powder, onion powder, cayenne pepper (if using), salt, and black pepper. Stir to combine.
    - In another shallow dish, whisk together the buttermilk and egg until well combined.
    - Place the breadcrumbs or cornmeal in a third shallow dish.
3. Bread the Pickles:
    - Dip each pickle slice into the flour mixture, coating both sides evenly and shaking off any excess flour.
    - Next, dip the floured pickle slice into the buttermilk mixture, allowing any excess to drip off.
    - Finally, coat the pickle slice in the breadcrumbs or cornmeal, pressing gently to adhere the coating to both sides. Place the breaded pickle slices on a baking sheet lined with parchment paper.
4. Fry the Pickles:

- In a deep skillet or Dutch oven, heat vegetable oil to 350°F (175°C) over medium-high heat.
- Carefully place the breaded pickle slices into the hot oil in batches, being careful not to overcrowd the pan. Fry for 2-3 minutes, or until golden brown and crispy.
- Use a slotted spoon or tongs to transfer the fried pickles to a paper towel-lined plate to drain excess oil. Repeat with the remaining pickle slices.

5. Serve:
   - Serve the fried pickles hot with ranch dressing, spicy mayo, or your favorite dipping sauce on the side.

Enjoy these crispy and flavorful fried pickles as a delicious appetizer or snack that's sure to be a hit at any gathering or game day party!

Cheese grits with shrimp

Ingredients:

For the cheese grits:

- 1 cup stone-ground grits
- 4 cups water or chicken broth
- 1 cup shredded cheddar cheese
- 2 tablespoons unsalted butter
- Salt and pepper to taste

For the shrimp:

- 1 pound large shrimp, peeled and deveined
- 2 cloves garlic, minced
- 2 tablespoons olive oil
- Salt and pepper to taste
- 1/2 teaspoon paprika
- 1/4 teaspoon cayenne pepper (optional, for heat)
- 2 tablespoons fresh lemon juice
- Chopped fresh parsley or green onions for garnish

Instructions:

1. Prepare the Cheese Grits:
    - In a medium saucepan, bring the water or chicken broth to a boil over high heat.
    - Gradually whisk in the grits, stirring constantly to prevent lumps from forming.
    - Reduce the heat to low and simmer, stirring occasionally, until the grits are thickened and creamy, about 20-25 minutes.
    - Stir in the shredded cheddar cheese and butter until melted and well combined. Season with salt and pepper to taste. Keep warm while preparing the shrimp.
2. Cook the Shrimp:

- In a large skillet, heat the olive oil over medium-high heat. Add the minced garlic and cook for 1 minute, until fragrant.
- Season the shrimp with salt, pepper, paprika, and cayenne pepper (if using). Add the seasoned shrimp to the skillet in a single layer.
- Cook the shrimp for 2-3 minutes per side, or until they are pink and opaque.
- Drizzle the lemon juice over the cooked shrimp and toss to coat.

3. Assemble the Dish:
   - Divide the cheese grits among serving bowls or plates.
   - Top the cheese grits with the cooked shrimp and any pan juices.
   - Garnish with chopped fresh parsley or green onions for added flavor and color.

4. Serve:
   - Serve the cheese grits with shrimp immediately, while hot.
   - Enjoy this delicious Southern-inspired dish as a main course for brunch, lunch, or dinner!

Cheese grits with shrimp is a comforting and flavorful dish that's perfect for any occasion. The creamy grits and tender shrimp pair perfectly together for a satisfying meal that will leave you craving more!

BBQ pulled chicken

Ingredients:

- 2 lbs boneless, skinless chicken breasts or thighs
- 1 cup barbecue sauce (use your favorite brand or homemade)
- 1/2 cup chicken broth or water
- 2 cloves garlic, minced
- 1 tablespoon brown sugar
- 1 tablespoon Worcestershire sauce
- 1 teaspoon smoked paprika
- 1/2 teaspoon onion powder
- Salt and pepper to taste

Instructions:

1. Season the chicken with salt, pepper, smoked paprika, and onion powder.
2. In a bowl, mix together the barbecue sauce, chicken broth or water, minced garlic, brown sugar, and Worcestershire sauce.
3. Place the seasoned chicken in a slow cooker or Instant Pot.
4. Pour the barbecue sauce mixture over the chicken, ensuring it's evenly coated.

For a slow cooker: Cook on low for 6-8 hours or high for 3-4 hours, until the chicken is tender and easily shreddable.

5. For an Instant Pot: Close the lid, set the valve to sealing, and cook on high pressure for 10 minutes. Allow natural release for 5 minutes, then quick release.
6. Once cooked, remove the chicken from the cooker and shred it using two forks.
7. Return the shredded chicken to the cooker and mix it well with the sauce.
8. Serve the BBQ Pulled Chicken on buns or sliders, topped with extra barbecue sauce if desired. Enjoy!

This recipe can be easily customized by adjusting the seasoning or adding ingredients like smoked paprika for extra flavor or a splash of hot sauce for some heat.